California Wine Winners

1991

Results of the 1990 Wine Judgings

Edited by
TRUDY AHLSTROM
and
J.T. DEVINE

ISBN 0-9614025-7-1
ISSN 0883-4423

To order additional copies of this book or
copies of the 1983, 1984, 1985, 1986, 1987, 1988 or 1989
editions, please send $5.95 plus 36¢ sales tax
for each book and $1.50 handling to:

VARIETAL FAIR
4022 Harrison Grade Road
Sebastopol, CA 95472
707 • 874 • 3105

TABLE OF CONTENTS

Los Angeles County Fair
Orange County Fair
Riverside Farmers Fair
San Francisco Fair
Dallas Morning News
California State Fair
National Orange Show
West Coast Competition
San Diego Competition

Cabernet Sauvignon
Chardonnay
Chenin Blanc
Gewurztraminer
Johannisberg Riesling
Meritage Red
Meritage White
Merlot
Petite Sirah
Pinot Noir
Sauvignon (Fume) Blanc
Sparkling Wine
White Zinfandel
Zinfandel

The purpose of this book is to provide one pocket-size guide to all the California wines that won medals in this year's competitions. The nine competitions covered and the twelve varietals included are listed on the facing page.

ORGANIZATION

The book is divided into two parts. The first part lists the award winners under specific varietals. Each varietal section is subdivided into groups of nine award winners, eight award winners, seven award winners, etc. The wineries are listed alphabetically within those subdivisions, and identified by vintage, appellation and price. Across from each wine a **G** (gold), **S** (silver), or **B** (bronze) shows what award was won in each of the competitions.

Johannisberg Riesling, Gewurztraminer and Sparkling Wines are further broken down into residual sugar classes, with higher residual sugar wines preceded by "R.S.___"

The second part of the book is an alphabetical listing of all the winning wineries including their addresses. Under each name, the winning wines are listed with the number of awards indicated in parenthesis so they can be easily found in the front section. Single-medal winners are listed only in the back, with the award and competition identified.

COMPETITIONS

The competitions start in January and last until August. Some wines can't be entered in all the judgings simply because the January entries are sold out by the end of summer. Some wineries, for whatever reason, choose not to enter their wines in competition. The entry requirements for the competitions vary, as do the categories within which they choose to judge. That information is summarized on the following page.

POINT COUNTS & REGION COMPARISONS

This year we have added a page at the beginning of each section that ranks the top dozen or so winners by weighting the value of each award. Gold = 5 points, Silver = 3 points, and Bronze = 1. The values are arbitrary; it is just another way of looking at the awards. Also included is a graph that shows which regions of the state took how many points of those weighted medals. The regions refer to those areas where the grapes were grown, not necessarily where the wineries are located:

North Coast ....Lake, Mendocino, Marin and Solano Counties.

Sonoma ....Sonoma County (11 Appellations).

Napa ....Napa County (5 Appellations).

Bay Area ....Santa Clara, Santa Cruz, Alameda Counties.

No. Central Coast ....Monterey and San Benito Counties.

So. Central Coast .....San Luis Obispo and Santa Barbara Counties.

South Coast .............L.A., Orange, Riverside, San Diego and Ventura Counties.

Sierra Foothills ....Amador, Calaveras, El Dorado, Nevada, Placer and Tuolomne Counties.

Other ....All other California Counties

California ....Non-specified blends from above appellations.

COMPETITION JUDGING DATES	ENTRIES # Wineries # in Calif. #Wines	MEDALS Total # in this book	ENTRY REQUIREMENTS AND RESTRICTIONS
LOS ANGELES COUNTY FAIR July 25 - 28	317 1500	405 287	All wines from any California winery; 1 wine per class.
ORANGE COUNTY FAIR June 2 - 3	? 2408	832 659	All California wines available in Orange County. 1 entry per class Judged in three price categories.
FARMERS FAIR RIVERSIDE May 5 - 6	264 1390	468 352	Any bonded winery in California. Limit of 15 entries.
SAN FRANCISCO FAIR June 12 - 14	417 294-CA 1925	537 374	Any U.S. wine.. Not all entries voluntary.
DALLAS MORNING NEWS Feb. 2 - 4	350 250-CA 1413	544 328	Any U.S. wine. Limit of 3 entries per category.
CALIFORNIA STATE FAIR July 6 - 8	413 1843	596 450	All California wine. Limit of 2 entries per class. Wines judged in 10 geographical groupings.
NATIONAL ORANGE SHOW March 1 - 2	320 237-CA 1501	458 266	Any U.S. wine. No limit on number of entries.
WEST COAST COMPETITION May 16 - 18	300 258-CA 1210	372 313	Any wine from the Western U.S. and Canada.
SAN DIEGO COMPETITION May 12 - 13	460 380-CA 1875	597 453	Any U.S.vinifera wine. No limit on number of entries.

LOLONIS

1986

Mendocino County

CABERNET SAUVIGNON

Lolonis Vineyards

PRIVATE RESERVE

PRODUCED AND BOTTLED BY LOLONIS
LAKEPORT, CALIFORNIA, U.S.A. • ALCOHOL 12.5% BY VOLUME

Cabernet Sauvignon

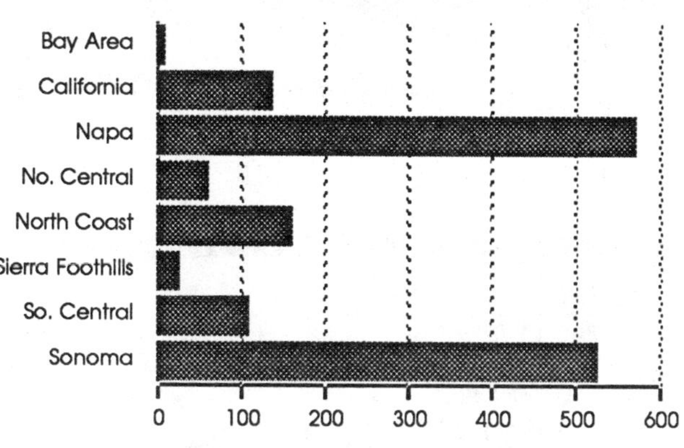

Regional Comparison of Total Points
(Gold=5   Silver=3   Bronze=1)

Highest   individual   wine   totals

2 2 GRGICH HILLS CELLAR
'85, Napa Vly. $20.00

2 1 LOLONIS WINERY
'86, Mendocino Co., Reserve $15.00

2 0 BRAREN PAULI WINERY
'87, Mauritson Vnyd. $11.50

2 0 RODNEY STRONG VINEYARDS
'85, Alexander's Crown Vnyd. $16.00

1 9 FETZER VINEYARDS
'85, Sonoma Co., Reserve $24.00

1 8 GARY FARRELL WINES
'87, Sonoma Co. $16.00

1 8 MARKHAM VINEYARDS
'85, Napa Vly $13.50

1 7 MONT ST. JOHN CELLARS
'85, Napa Vly. $14.00

1 7 SEQUOIA GROVE VINEYARDS
'87, Napa Vly., Estate $22.00

1 5 FETZER VINEYARDS
'86, Mendocino, Barrel Select $12.00

1 5 KENDALL-JACKSON WINERY
'86, California, Cardinale $15.00

	L.A.	Orange	Farmers	San Fran	Dallas	State Fair	Nat'l O.S.	W. Coast	San Diego
7 AWARDS									
FETZER VINEYARDS '86, Mendocino, Barrel Select $12.00		B	G	S		S	B	B	B
MONT ST. JOHN CELLARS '85, Napa Vly. $14.00	B	B	G			S	S	B	S
6 AWARDS									
BAREFOOT CELLARS 'NV, California $4.99	B		B			B	B	B	B
BRAREN PAULI WINERY '87, Dry Creek Vly., Mauritson Vnyd. $11.50		G	B	G	S		S	S	
CLOS DU VAL WINE CO. '86, Napa Vly., Estate $16.00		B	S	B		S	S	B	
COSENTINO CRYSTAL VALLEY '87, North Coast/Sonoma Co. $14.00	S	B		S		B		S	S
DOMAINE MICHEL '86, Sonoma Co. $19.50		S	S	S		B		B	B
GARY FARRELL WINES '87, Sonoma Co. $16.00	S	G	G		S			B	B
GRGICH HILLS CELLAR '85, Napa Vly. $20.00	G	G	B	S			G		S
GUNDLACH BUNDSCHU WINERY '86, Sonoma Vly., Rhinefarm Vnyds. $12.00		S	S		B	B		B	B
WILLIAM HILL WINERY '86, Napa Vly., Reserve $24.00	B		B	B	B	B		S	
MARKHAM VINEYARDS '85, Napa Vly $13.50	S		G			B	G	S	B
RODNEY STRONG VINEYARDS '85, Alexander's Crown Vnyd. $16.00	S	G	S			S		B	G
5 AWARDS									
BARGETTO WINERY '87, Napa Vly., Cypress $9.75		G	S			B		B	S
ESTANCIA '87, Alexander Vly. $8.00		B	B		B	B			B
FETZER VINEYARDS '85, Sonoma Co., Reserve $24.00	S	G	S			S			G
GUENOC WINERY '86, Lake Co.	B	B				S	G	S	
HACIENDA WINERY '85, Sonoma Co. $14.00		S	S		B	B			G

Cabernet Sauvignon

San Diego	W. Coast	Nat'l O.S.	State Fair	Dallas	San Fran	Farmers	Orange	L.A.	
									5 AWARDS
S	G		B		S		B		**HUSCH VINEYARDS** '87, Mendocino, La Ribera Vnyd. $12.00
B				B	G		S	G	**KENDALL-JACKSON WINERY** '86, California, Cardinale $15.00
S				B	S		B	G	**KENDALL-JACKSON WINERY** '86, California, Vintner's Reserve $14.00
S				S	B	B	B		**KENDALL-JACKSON WINERY** '86, California, Proprietor's $24.00
		S		G	S	G	G		**LOLONIS WINERY** '86, Mendocino, Private Reserve $15.00
B	S			S		S	B		**MONTICELLO CELLARS** '87, Napa Vly., Jefferson Cuvee $14.00
B	B		S		B		B		**A. RAFANELLI WINERY** '87, Dry Creek Vly. $11.50
	B		B		B	S		B	**V. SATTUI WINERY** '86, Napa Vly. $12.95
B	G	G				G	B		**SEQUOIA GROVE VINEYARDS** '87, Napa Vly., Estate $22.00
B	S		B			B	S		**RODNEY STRONG VINEYARDS** '87, Sonoma Co. $9.00
B		G	B		S		B		**VALLEY OF THE MOON WINERY** '87, Sonoma Vly., Reserve $12.00
B					B	B	S	S	**WENTE BROS.** '87, Napa Vly. $8.00
									4 AWARDS
		B		S		B		S	**BEAULIEU VINEYARD** '85, Napa Vly., DeLatour, Reserve $27.00
		G		S	S	S			**BEL ARBORS** 'NV, American, Founder's Sel. $5.49
			B	S			G	B	**BLACK MOUNTAIN VINEYARD** '85, Alexander Vly. $18.00
	B	S	B			S			**J. CAREY CELLARS** '86, Santa Ynez, La Cuesta Vnyd. $13.00
B			G	G			B		**CLOS DU BOIS WINES** '87, Alexander Vly. $12.00
B		G			B			G	**CONN CREEK WINERY** '85, Napa Vly. $13.00

Cabernet Sauvignon

4 AWARDS

	L.A.	Orange	Farmers	San Fran	Dallas	State Fair	Nat'l O.S.	W. Coast	San Diego
COSENTINO CRYSTAL VALLEY '87, North Coast $16.00		S	S	B					G
FREMONT CREEK '86, Mendocino/Napa $9.50		B			B	G		S	
GOLDEN CREEK VINEYARD '87, Sonoma Co. $10.50		G	B		S				S
HANNA WINERY '87, Sonoma Co. $16.00		B	B	B					S
HESS COLLECTION WINERY '86, Napa Vly. $14.25		B	B	B		S			
CHARLES KRUG WINERY '84, Napa Vly., Vintage Selection $20.00	B		B			G	G		
CHARLES KRUG WINERY '85, Napa Vly. $10.50		G			S	S			S
LOUIS M. MARTINI '87, Napa Vly., Reserve $12.99		S	B		G				B
PAUL MASSON VINEYARDS '86, Monterey Co. $8.00				B	B		B	B	
MONTEREY PENINSULA WINERY '84, Monterey, Doctor's Reserve $16.00					B	S	S		S
ROBERT PECOTA WINERY '87, Napa Vly., Kara's Vnyd. $16.00			S			B		B	G
SEBASTIANI VINEYARDS '85, Sonoma Co., Reserve $11.00				G	S			B	S
ST. FRANCIS WINERY '87, Sonoma Vly. $20.00		G	B			S	S		
ST. SUPERY VINEYARDS '87, Napa Vly., Dollarhide Ranch					S		G	B	B
WHITEHALL LANE WINERY '86, Napa Vly. $16.00		G				S	S		B
WHITEHALL LANE WINERY '87, Napa $16.00	G	S		S					B
WILD HORSE WINERY '86, Central Coast $12.00			B		S	B		B	
WILD HORSE WINERY '87, Paso Robles $12.00		B		G				S	B
WINDSOR VINEYARDS '84, Mendocino Co. $9.00				S		B	G		B

Cabernet Sauvignon

San Diego	W. Coast	Nat'l O.S.	State Fair	Dallas	San Fran	Farmers	Orange	L.A.	
									4 AWARDS
B		S	B				B		**WINDSOR VINEYARDS** '85, Russian River Vly., Reserve $12.00
									3 AWARDS
B	B		S						**BALVERNE WINERY** '84, Chalk Hill, Laurel Vnyd. $12.00
S			G			G			**BENZIGER OF GLEN ELLEN** '87, Sonoma Co. $10.00
	B		G				S		**CHATEAU JULIEN** '86, Monterey Co., Reserve $17.00
	G				B		B		**CHATEAU ST. JEAN** '86, Alexander Vly. $19.00
	S		S			B			**CHRISTIAN BROTHERS** '86, Napa Vly. $10.00
			S			S	B		**CLOS PEGASE WINERY** '86, Napa Vly. $17.00
B		S					B		**COSENTINO CRYSTAL VALLEY** '86, North Coast, Reserve
			S	B	B				**CRESTON MANOR VINEYARD** '86, Paso Robles, Winemaker's Sel. $19.50
	B			B			B		**DUNNEWOOD VINEYARDS** '86, Napa Vly., Reserve
			S				G	B	**GLEN ELLEN WINERY** '87, California, Proprietors Reserve $5.75
		G	S		B				**GRAND CRU VINEYARDS** '86, Alexander Vly., Reserve $22.00
B	B				B				**GRAND CRU VINEYARDS** '87, Sonoma Co. $12.00
			S		B	S			**HOP KILN WINERY** '86, Dry Creek Vly. $12.00
G		S				B			**INGLENOOK NAPA VALLEY** '85, Napa, Estate Reserve Cask $16.00
G					G		S		**LAMBERT BRIDGE** '87, Dry Creek Vly., Library Reserve $15.00
	B			S			B		**J. LOHR WINERY** '87, California
B			B			B			**LOUIS M. MARTINI** '87, Sonoma Co. $9.45

Cabernet Sauvignon

	L.A.	Orange	Farmers	San Fran	Dallas	State Fair	Nat'l O.S.	W. Coast	San Diego
MOUNT PALOMAR WINERY '85, Dry Creek Vly. $10.00		S	S				G		
MURPHY-GOODE WINERY '87, Alexander Vly., Premier Vnyd. $16.50			B			S			G
NAVARRO VINEYARDS '85, Mendocino $14.00			S				S		B
OLSON WINERY '86, Mendocino Co. $10.00			S			B			B
PALISADES VINEYARDS '86, Napa Vly., Reserve $9.00		B		B	B				
J. PEDRONCELLI WINERY '82, Dry Creek Vly., Reserve	B	S							B
PEJU PROVINCE WINERY '87, Napa Vly., HB Vnyd. $20.00		S		S				G	
QUIVIRA VINEYARDS '87, Dry Creek Vly. $14.50			S			S	G		
RABBIT RIDGE VINEYARDS '86, Russian River Vly. $12.00			B				S	S	
ROUND HILL CELLARS '87, Napa Vly.	G	G							S
ROUND HILL CELLARS 'NV, California, House, Lot 7 $5.49		B	B	B					
V. SATTUI WINERY '87, Napa Vly., Preston Vnyd. $16.95			S		G				B
SHAFER VINEYARDS '87, Napa Vly., Stag's Leap Dist. $17.00		S	B	S					
STELZNER VINEYARDS '86, Napa Vly., Estate $16.00						S	B		B
VILLA MT. EDEN WINERY '85, Napa Vly., Estate $12.00					B	B			B
VINA VISTA VINEYARDS '85, Alexander Vly., Reserve	G				S				G
WINDSOR VINEYARDS '86, Russian River Vly., Reserve $12.00			S				B		S
ZACA MESA WINERY '87, Central Coast, Reserve $18.00		S		G		G			
ZD WINES '86, Napa Vly. $16.00		B				B			B

Cabernet Sauvignon

2 AWARDS

San Diego	W. Coast	Nat'l O.S.	State Fair	Dallas	San Fran	Farmers	Orange	L.A.	
S							B		**ALEXANDER VALLEY VINEYARDS** '87, Wetzel Family Vnyd., Estate
	B						S		**VINCENT ARROYO WINERY** '87, Napa Vly., Estate
B						S			**BANDIERA WINERY** '86, Napa Vly. $6.50
B			B						**BARGETTO WINERY** '88, California Cabernet Table Wine $5.50
			B			B			**BEAULIEU VINEYARD** '86, Napa Vly., Rutherford $9.50
		S		G					**BENZIGER OF GLEN ELLEN** '86, Sonoma Vly., Estate
S								G	**BENZIGER OF GLEN ELLEN** '87, Sonoma Co., Estate
							B	G	**BRAREN PAULI WINERY** '87, Mendocino
			B			S			**BRUTOCAO** '86, Mendocino $9.00
			S			B			**BUENA VISTA WINERY** '86, Carneros, Reserve $22.50
B							S		**BURGESS CELLARS** '86, Napa Vly., Vintage Selection
				S			G		**CASTORO CELLARS** '87, Paso Robles, Hope Farms
B				B					**CHATEAU JULIEN** '82, Monterey Co., Reserve $17.00
G				G					**CHATEAU SOUVERAIN** '86, Alexander Vly.
	S						S		**CLOS DU BOIS WINES** '86, Alexander Vly., Briarcrest
						B	G		**CORBETT CANYON VINEYARDS** '87, Central Coast, Reserve $8.50
				B			G		**CRESTON MANOR VINEYARD** '86, San Luis Obispo Co. $10.00
	B						B		**DEER VALLEY VINEYARDS** '86, California
						S	G		**DEHLINGER WINERY** '86, Russian River Vly., Estate $13.00

2 AWARDS

	L.A.	Orange	Farmers	San Fran	Dallas	State Fair	Nat'l O.S.	W. Coast	San Diego
DRY CREEK VINEYARD '87, Sonoma Co.					S			S	
DURNEY VINEYARD '83, Carmel Vly., Reserve $20.00				B		G			
ESTRELLA RIVER WINERY '85, Paso Robles $12.00		B		B					
FENESTRA CELLARS '86, Monterey, Smith & Hook Vnyd. $13.50		G				S			
FETZER VINEYARDS '87, California		G			B				
FIELD STONE WINERY '85, Alexander Vly., Hoot Owl Creek		B						B	
FIRESTONE VINEYARD '87, Santa Ynez Vly.		B						B	
THOMAS FOGARTY WINERY '84, Napa Vly. $15.50						B			B
FRANCISCAN OAKVILLE ESTATE '85, Napa Vly., Reserve $15.00		S	S						
FRANCISCAN OAKVILLE ESTATE '86, Napa Vly., Library Selection		B						S	
GAN EDEN WINERY '86, Alexander Vly.		B					G		
GEYSER PEAK WINERY '86, Alexander Vly., Estate								B	B
GEYSER PEAK WINERY '87, Sonoma Co.		S						S	
RICHARD L. GRAESER WINERY '86, Napa Vly.						B		S	
GRANITE SPRINGS WINERY '87, El Dorado Co., Estate		B							S
GUENOC WINERY '85, Guenoc Vly., Premier Cuvee $17.00						B			S
GUGLIELMO WINERY '85, Santa Clara Vly., Reserve $10.00				B					S
HALLCREST VINEYARDS '87, El Dorado, De Cascabel Vnyd. $11.00			S						B
KENWOOD WINERY '86, Sonoma Vly.		S		S					

Cabernet Sauvignon

2 AWARDS

San Diego	W. Coast	Nat'l O.S.	State Fair	Dallas	San Fran	Farmers	Orange	L.A.	
			B				G		**KENWOOD WINERY** '87, Sonoma Vly., Jack London Vnyd. $18.00
B						B			**CHARLES KRUG WINERY** '83, Napa Vly., Vintage Selection $20.00
	B						S		**LEEWARD WINERY** '86, Alexander Vly.
		G			G				**J. LOHR WINERY** '85, Napa, Carol's Vnyd., Reserve $17.50
G				G					**J. LOHR WINERY** '85, Napa Vly., Carol's Vnyd., Lot 2
							G	S	**LYTTON SPRINGS WINERY** '87, Mendocino Co., Reserve
				G	B				**MAZZOCCO VINEYARDS** '87, Alexander Vly. $20.00
							B	G	**MIRASSOU VINEYARDS** '85, Napa, Fifth Generation Reserve
			S				S		**MIRASSOU VINEYARDS** '86, California, Fifth Generation Sel. $9.00
B							S		**ROBERT MONDAVI WINERY** '86, Napa Vly., Reserve
				S			S		**MONT ST. JOHN CELLARS** '84, Napa Vly. $14.00
		G				B			**MONTEREY VINEYARD** '86, Monterey Co., Ltd. Release
			B				S		**MOUNT VEEDER WINERY** '86, Napa Vly., Mt. Veeder Vnyd. $18.00
	S					B			**NAPA RIDGE WINERY** '87, North Coast
	B						G		**NEVADA CITY WINERY** '87, Sierra Foothills
					B	B			**GUSTAVE NIEBAUM COLLECTION** '86, Napa Vly., Tench Vnyd. $14.00
B			S						**ED OLIVEIRA WINERY** '86, Knights Vly. $12.00
B	S								**PAT PAULSEN VINEYARDS** '85, Sonoma Co.

Cabernet Sauvignon

2 AWARDS

	L.A.	Orange	Farmers	San Fran	Dallas	State Fair	Nat'l O.S.	W. Coast	San Diego
PESENTI WINERY '88, Paso Robles, Family Reserve $10.00			S			S			
POPPY HILL CELLARS '86, California $6.99		B	S						
BERNARD PRADEL CELLARS '86, Napa Vly.		G							B
PRESTON VINEYARDS '87, Dry Creek Vly. $12.00						B		S	
RAYMOND VINEYARD '85, Napa Vly., Reserve $24.00				B					S
RUTHERFORD RANCH '85, Rutherford Ranch $10.50			B		B				
RUTHERFORD VINTNERS '78, Napa Vly. $22.50	S					S			
SANTA BARBARA WINERY '87, Santa Ynez Vly., Reserve	G	B							
SEBASTIANI VINEYARDS '87, Sonoma Co. $8.00	S					B			
SEGHESIO WINERY '86, Northern Sonoma Co.		S					B		
SEQUOIA GROVE VINEYARDS '86, Napa $16.00				B		S			
SEQUOIA GROVE VINEYARDS '87, Napa Co. $16.00				B			G		
SMITH & HOOK WINERY '85, Monterey Co.		B						G	
ST. CLEMENT VINEYARDS '85, Napa Vly. $17.00			B						S
STERLING VINEYARDS '86, Napa, Diamond Mt. Ranch $16.00		B				B			
STEVENOT WINERY '85, Calaveras Co., Grand Reserve						B	S		
RODNEY STRONG VINEYARDS '84, Alexander's Crown						B	B		
SWANSON WINERY '87, Napa Vly. $18.50			G	S					
TULOCAY WINERY '87, Napa Vly.	B								S

Cabernet Sauvignon

San Diego	W. Coast	Nat'l O.S.	State Fair	Dallas	San Fran	Farmers	Orange	L.A.	
						2 AWARDS			
			B				S		**M. G. VALLEJO WINERY** '87, California $5.75
	S				S				**VICHON WINERY** '87, Napa Vly., Stags Leap Dist. $23.00
							B	G	**WEIBEL VINEYARDS** '87, Mendocino Co.
		G						S	**WHITEHALL LANE WINERY** 'NV, California, Le Petite
		S		S					**J. WILE & SONS** '87, Napa Vly.
S						S			**WINDSOR VINEYARDS** '85, Mendocino Co., Haehl Ranch $9.00
			G				B		**WOODSIDE VINEYARDS** '87, Santa Cruz Mtns. Estate $15.00

1988
White Oak
Sonoma County

Chardonnay

MYERS LIMITED RESERVE

142 of 988 cases *Bill Myers*

PRODUCED AND BOTTLED BY
WHITE OAK VINEYARDS & WINERY, HEALDSBURG, CA.
ALC. 12.8% BY VOL. CONTAINS SULFITES

DE LOACH VINEYARDS

SONOMA COUNTY
RUSSIAN RIVER VALLEY
CHARDONNAY
1988

PRODUCED & BOTTLED BY DE LOACH VINEYARDS INC.
SANTA ROSA, SONOMA COUNTY, CALIFORNIA, USA
ALCOHOL 13.5% BY VOLUME • CONTAINS SULFITES

Chardonnay

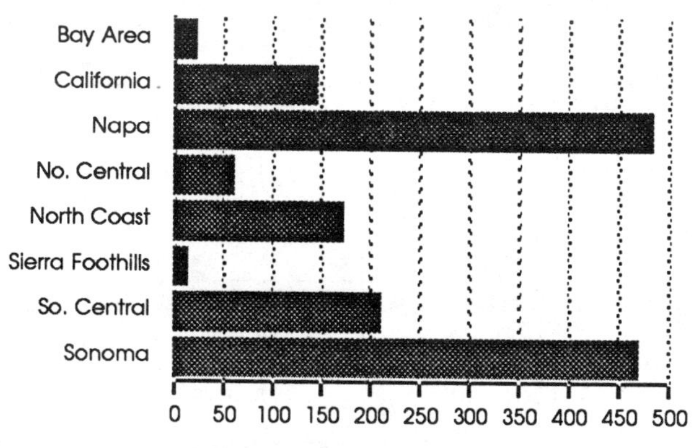

Regional Comparison of Total Points

(Gold=5   Silver=3   Bronze=1)

Highest individual wine totals

2 6   **KENDALL-JACKSON WINERY**
'88, California, Proprietor's $22.50

2 5   **WHITE OAK VINEYARDS**
'88, Sonoma Co., Reserve $20.00

2 1   **DE LOACH VINEYARDS**
'88, Russian River Vly. $15.00

1 9   **WILLIAM HILL WINERY**
'88, Napa Vly., Reserve $18.00

1 9   **WHITE OAK VINEYARDS**
'88, Sonoma Co. $12.00

1 8   **HANDLEY CELLARS**
'87, Anderson Vly. $11.00

1 8   **HESS COLLECTION WINERY**
'88, Napa Vly. $13.75

1 7   **BENZIGER OF GLEN ELLEN**
'88, Sonoma Co. $10.00

1 7   **GAN EDEN WINERY**
'88, Sonoma Co.,/Napa Vly. $12.00

1 7   **HIDDEN CELLARS**
'89, Mendocino, Tillman Vnyd. $16.00

1 7   **LEEWARD WINERY**
'89, Central Coast $11.00

1 7   **MERIDIAN VINEYARDS**
'88, Santa Barbara Co. $9.00

Chardonnay

	L.A.	Orange	Farmers	San Fran	Dallas	State Fair	Nat'l O.S.	W. Coast	San Diego
8 AWARDS									
HESS COLLECTION WINERY '88, Napa Vly. $13.75	G	B	B	S	B		B	B	G
WILLIAM HILL WINERY '88, Napa Vly., Reserve $18.00	S	G	B	S	S	B		G	S
KENDALL-JACKSON WINERY '88, California, The Proprietor's $22.50		G	S	B	S	S	G	B	G
7 AWARDS									
HUSCH VINEYARDS '88, Mendocino Co., Estate $11.00	S			G	S	B	B	B	B
KENDALL-JACKSON WINERY '89, California, Vintner's Reserve $12.50	S	B	G	B		B		B	B
WHITE OAK VINEYARDS '88, Sonoma Co., Reserve $20.00	G	G	S	G	B	B		G	
6 AWARDS									
CLOS DU BOIS WINES '87, Alexander Vly., Reserve $24.00		S	S	B	B		S		B
HANDLEY CELLARS '87, Anderson Vly. $11.00	B	S	G		S			B	G
LOLONIS WINERY '88, Mendocino Co., Reserve $18.00		S	B	G	S	B	B		
NAVARRO VINEYARDS '88, Mendocino $9.75	B	S		B		S	B	S	
TAFT STREET WINERY '89, Sonoma Co. $8.50	S	S	B	B		B			S
5 AWARDS									
BENZIGER OF GLEN ELLEN '88, Sonoma Co. $10.00			G		S		G	S	B
CAMBRIA WINERY '88, Santa Maria Vly., Reserve $25.00	B	G		B		B			S
CHAPPELLET VINEYARD '87, Napa Vly. $14.00		B	B		S			S	G
CLOS PEGASE WINERY '87, Napa Vly. $13.00		G	S		B		S		B
CLOS PEGASE WINERY '87, Los Carneros $15.50			B		G	B	S		B
DE LOACH VINEYARDS '88, Russian River Vly. $15.00	S			S	G			G	G

San Diego	W. Coast	Nat'l O.S.	State Fair	Dallas	San Fran	Farmers	Orange	L.A.	
5 AWARDS									
B	S		S	S			B		**DEHLINGER WINERY** '88, Russian River Vly., Estate $12.00
			B	S		B	S	B	**FRITZ CELLARS** '88, Russian River Vly. $12.50
S		G	S		G			B	**GAN EDEN WINERY** '88, Sonoma Co./Napa Vly. $12.00
	G	B	S			S		S	**GLEN ELLEN WINERY** '88, Sangiacomo Vnyd., Imagery $16.00
	S		B		B	G		G	**GREENWOOD RIDGE VINEYARDS** '89, Mendocino, Lolonis Vnyd. $13.50
	G		B	S	S		B		**HANDLEY CELLARS** '88, Dry Creek Vly. $14.50
	B	B	B				S	B	**HIDDEN CELLARS** '88, Mendocino Co. $12.00
B	G		S		S		G		**HIDDEN CELLARS** '89, Mendocino, Tillman Vnyd. $16.00
B	S				B	B	B		**KONOCTI WINERY** '88, Lake Co. $9.00
G					B	G	B	G	**LEEWARD WINERY** '89, Central Coast $11.00
		S	G		S	S	S		**MERIDIAN VINEYARDS** '88, Santa Barbara Co. $9.00
B			B		S	G	S		**MOUNT VEEDER WINERY** '88, Napa Vly. $16.00
B	B			G		G	B		**RABBIT RIDGE VINEYARDS** '88, Russian River Vly. $14.00
B	G			S	S			B	**TREFETHEN VINEYARDS** '87, Napa, Estate $16.75
	B		B	B	B		G		**VICHON WINERY** '88, Napa Vly. $16.00
S	S			G	S		G		**WHITE OAK VINEYARDS** '88, Sonoma Co. $12.00
B	G	G				B	B		**WINDSOR VINEYARDS** '87, Russian River, River Estates $11.00
4 AWARDS									
S	B			S			G		**BYRON VINEYARD** '88, Santa Barbara Co.

Chardonnay

	L.A.	Orange	Farmers	San Fran	Dallas	State Fair	Nat'l O.S.	W. Coast	San Diego
4 AWARDS									
CAMBRIA WINERY '89, Santa Maria, Katherines Vnyd. $16.00	G	B				B			G
CLOS DU BOIS WINES '88, Dry Creek Vly., Flintwood $18.00				S	S	S			B
DRY CREEK VINEYARD '89, Sonoma Co. $12.50				S	B	B		G	
GARY FARRELL WINES '88, Russian River Vly. $16.00				B	B	B		B	
FETZER VINEYARDS '88, Mendocino Co., Reserve $17.50				B	B		B	B	
FETZER VINEYARDS '88, Mendocino, Barrel Select $12.00		B			B			B	B
FLORA SPRINGS WINERY '88, Napa Vly $15.00		S			B	B		B	
FOLIE A DEUX WINERY '88, Napa Vly. $16.00				B	B			B	G
FRANCISCAN OAKVILLE ESTATE '88, Napa Vly. $12.00	S	S	S		S				
GRGICH HILLS CELLAR '87, Napa Vly. $22.00				S		B	G		S
LANDMARK VINEYARDS '87, Sonoma Co.		B				G	S	B	
MAZZOCCO VINEYARDS '88, Alexander Vly. $16.50	G	B		S		B			
NAVARRO VINEYARDS '88, Anderson Vly., Reserve $14.00		B			B		S		S
NEWTON VINEYARD '88, Napa Vly. $14.00		B			B		G		B
PARSONS CREEK WINERY '88, Sonoma Co., Winemakers $13.00		G	B	S		B			
SANTA BARBARA WINERY '88, Santa Ynez Vly., Reserve $18.00		B		S		G			G
STEVENOT WINERY '88, Calaveras, Grand Reserve $10.00		B		B	B			B	
RODNEY STRONG VINEYARDS '87, Sonoma, Chalk Hill Vnyd. $12.00		B					G	G	B
SWANSON WINERY '88, Napa Vly. $14.95				S		B	B	G	

Chardonnay

San Diego	W. Coast	Nat'l O.S.	State Fair	Dallas	San Fran	Farmers	Orange	L.A.	
									4 AWARDS
	S		B		B		S		**TAFT STREET WINERY** '88, Russian River Vly. $11.50
			S		S		S	B	**WINDSOR VINEYARDS** '88, Russian River, Preston Ranch $12.00
		B			B	B	B		**WINDSOR VINEYARDS** '88, Alexander, Murphy Ranch $10.00
	B		S			B	B		**ZD WINES** '88, California $20.00
									3 AWARDS
			B	S		B			**ADELAIDA CELLARS** '87, Paso Robles $12.75
			B	B			B		**ADELAIDA CELLARS** '88, Paso Robles $13.25
B	S			B					**ALDERBROOK VINEYARDS** '88, Dry Creek Vly.
			S				B	G	**BABCOCK VINEYARDS** '88, Santa Ynez Vly. $16.00
	B			G		G			**BARGETTO WINERY** '88, Santa Cruz Mtns. $18.00
B						S	S		**CAMBRIA WINERY** '88, Santa Barbara, Cambria $15.00
B	B		B						**J. CAREY CELLARS** '88, Santa Ynez Vly. $12.00
			B		B		G		**CHRISTIAN BROTHERS** '88, Napa $8.50
S				S	B				**CLOS DU BOIS WINES** '88, Alexander Vly., Calcaire $16.00
			B	B			S		**CORBETT CANYON VINEYARDS** '88, Central Coast, Reserve $8.25
S	B						S		**CRICHTON HALL ESTATE** '88, Napa Vly.
				B	S		G		**DOMAINE NAPA WINERY** '88, Napa Co. $12.50
				B		B	B		**EBERLE WINERY** '87, Paso Robles $12.00
		G				B	S		**FETZER VINEYARDS** '89, California, Sundial $7.49

Chardonnay

	L.A.	Orange	Farmers	San Fran	Dallas	State Fair	Nat'l O.S.	W. Coast	San Diego
3 AWARDS									
FLORA SPRINGS WINERY '88, Napa Vly, Barrel Ferm. $23.50				B		B			G
FRISINGER CELLARS '88, Napa, Estate $14.00				S	B			B	
GLEN ELLEN WINERY 'NV, California, Proprietors Res. $5.75		S				B			B
GRGICH HILLS CELLAR '88, Napa Vly. $22.00	G			B		G			
GUENOC WINERY '88, Guenoc Vly., Monogram Res.	S				B		S		
JEPSON VINEYARDS '87, Mendocino $12.50			B				B	B	
JORY WINERY '88, Monterey, La Reina, Res. $22.00			S	B			B		
J. LOHR WINERY '88, Monterey Co., Riverstone $12.00				B	S				S
MISSION VIEW VINEYARDS '88, Paso Robles, Estate $9.50					B	B			S
GUSTAVE NIEBAUM COLLECTION '88, Napa, Carneros, Laird Vnyd. $14.00	B	B		B					
PARSONS CREEK WINERY '87, Sonoma Co., Carneros $8.50			B		B			B	
ROBERT PEPI '88, Napa Vly. $15.00		S		B				S	
RABBIT RIDGE VINEYARDS '88, Sonoma Co.					B		B		B
SANTA BARBARA WINERY '88, Santa Ynez Vly.	S	B						S	
SCHUG CELLARS '87, Carneros, Beckstoffer Vnyd. $14.75						B		G	B
SEQUOIA GROVE VINEYARDS '88, Napa Vly., Estate	B					B			B
ST. ANDREWS WINERY '88, Napa Vly. $10.00	B	B		B					
ST. FRANCIS WINERY '88, California $10.00	S			B	G				
RODNEY STRONG VINEYARDS '88, Chalk Hill $12.00				B		B	B		

Chardonnay

3 AWARDS

San Diego	W. Coast	Nat'l O.S.	State Fair	Dallas	San Fran	Farmers	Orange	L.A.	
		S	B			B			**SWANSON WINERY** — '88, Napa Vly., Reserve $18.50
G			B				G		**VILLA ZAPU** — '88, Napa Vly. $15.00
S		B					S		**WINDSOR VINEYARDS** — '87, Russian River, Winemasters
B					S		B		**STEPHEN ZELLERBACH** — '88, Sonoma $8.00

2 AWARDS

San Diego	W. Coast	Nat'l O.S.	State Fair	Dallas	San Fran	Farmers	Orange	L.A.	
B		B							**S. ANDERSON VINEYARD** — '88, Stags Leap, Estate
		B				B			**AUDUBON CELLARS** — '87, Sonoma, Carneros, Sangiacomo $11.25
			B					G	**AUDUBON CELLARS** — '89, Napa Vly., Segas Vnyd., LH $10.99
	B		B						**BALVERNE WINERY** — '88, Chalk Hill $9.50
S	B								**BARGETTO WINERY** — '89, Central Coast, Cypress
B	G								**BEAULIEU VINEYARD** — '88, Carneros, Reserve
				B	S				**BELVEDERE WINERY** — '88, Carneros, Reserve $12.00
						S	B		**BERINGER VINEYARDS** — '88, Napa Vly., Estate Reserve $18.50
B			B						**BLACK MOUNTAIN VINEYARD** — '88, Alexander Vly., Douglas Hill $10.00
B	S								**BOUCHAINE VINEYARDS** — '87, Carneros $16.00
			B		S				**BOYER** — '88, Monterey, Ventana Vnyd. $13.50
B	B								**BRUTOCAO** — '88, Mendocino $9.00
	B			S					**BUENA VISTA WINERY** — '87, Carneros, Reserve
B					S				**DAVIS BYNUM WINERY** — '88, Russian River Vly. $16.00

Chardonnay

	L.A.	Orange	Farmers	San Fran	Dallas	State Fair	Nat'l O.S.	W. Coast	San Diego
2 AWARDS									
CAIN CELLARS '88, Napa Vly., Carneros $16.00				B		B			
CARNEROS CREEK WINERY '88, Los Carneros		S			B				
CHATEAU DE LEU WINERY '88, Green Vly., Solano, Estate $8.95						S			S
CHATEAU SOUVERAIN '87, Sonoma, Carneros, Reserve								S	G
CHATEAU SOUVERAIN '88, Sonoma, Carneros, Reserve $13.00		S		B					
CLOS DU BOIS WINES '88, Alexander Vly. $12.00				S				S	
CLOS DU VAL WINE CO. '88, Napa Vly., Carneros, Estate $14.00						B	B		
CONGRESS SPRINGS VINEYARDS '88, San Ysidro, Reserve		S							B
CONGRESS SPRINGS VINEYARDS '88, Santa Clara Co. $12.50					B	B			
CORBETT CANYON VINEYARDS '88, Central Coast, Classic $15.00		S	B						
COSENTINO CRYSTAL VALLEY '89, North Coast/Napa Co. $14.00	S					S			
CRESTON MANOR VINEYARD '88, Paso Robles						B			S
DE LORIMER WINERY '88, Alexander Vly., Prism $13.50		G				B			
DELICATO VINEYARDS '88, California $6.50	S		B						
DRY CREEK VINEYARD '87, Dry Creek Vly., Reserve $18.00		S							G
ESTANCIA '88, Monterey $8.00		S					B		
FENESTRA CELLARS '88, Monterey, La Riena Vnyd. $12.50				G	S				
FILSINGER VINEYARDS '89, Barrel Fermented $8.00	B		B						
FRANCISCAN OAKVILLE ESTATE '88, Napa, Cuvee Sauvage		G		S					

Chardonnay

2 AWARDS

San Diego	W. Coast	Nat'l O.S.	State Fair	Dallas	San Fran	Farmers	Orange	L.A.	
B							S		**FREEMARK ABBEY WINERY** '88, Napa Vly, Carpy Ranch
					S		S		**FRITZ CELLARS** '88, Dry Creek Vly. $9.50
B			B						**GAUER ESTATE** '88, Alexander Vly. $16.00
		B						B	**GUNDLACH BUNDSCHU WINERY** '88, Sonoma Vly.
						B	B		**HALLCREST VINEYARDS** '88, California, Fortuyn Cuvee $9.00
		B					S		**HAYWOOD WINERY** '88, Sonoma, Los Chamizal $14.50
B		G							**BARON HERZOG WINE CELLARS** '89, Sonoma Co.
						B	S		**HOP KILN WINERY** '89, Russian Riv., M. Griffin Vnyds.
		S			B				**INGLENOOK NAPA VALLEY** '87, Napa Vly., Reserve $15.00
B		S							**JEKEL VINEYARDS** '86, Arroyo Seco, Gravelstone
B				S					**JEKEL VINEYARDS** '86, Arroyo Seco, Estate $20.00
			S		B				**JUSTIN VINEYARDS** '88, Paso Robles $13.50
			B		B				**KENWOOD WINERY** '88, Sonoma, Beltane Ranch $13.00
			B	B					**LA REINA WINERY** '87, Monterey $13.50
				B			S		**LAMBERT BRIDGE** '87, Dry Creek Vly.
				S	B				**LAMBERT BRIDGE** '88, Dry Creek, Tete De Cuvee $22.00
						S	S		**MARIO PERELLI-MINETTI** '88, Napa Vly.
					B	S			**MARK WEST VINEYARDS** '87, Russian Riv., Le Beau Vnyds. $12.00
B						B			**MARTIN BROTHERS WINERY** '89, Paso Robles, Estate $10.00

Chardonnay

	L.A.	Orange Farmers	San Fran	Dallas	State Fair	Nat'l O.S.	W. Coast	San Diego
2 AWARDS								
MIRASSOU VINEYARDS '88, Monterey, 5th Generation Res.	B	B						
MISSION VIEW VINEYARDS '89, Paso Robles, Estate $9.50	S				B			
ROBERT MONDAVI WINERY '88, Napa Vly. $16.00		B	S					
MONT ST. JOHN CELLARS '88, Napa, Carneros, Estate $12.75			B					B
MURPHY-GOODE WINERY '89, Alexander Vly. $12.00	S				S			
NAPA CREEK WINERY '88, Napa Vly. $15.00			B	B				
NAPA RIDGE WINERY '89, Central Coast		S						S
JOSEPH PHELPS VINEYARDS '89, California $7.00		G	B					
REVERE VINEYARDS '88, Napa, Reserve $22.00	B		B					
ROUND HILL CELLARS '88, Napa Vly., Reserve $8.75		B			B			
SAINTSBURY WINERY '88, Carneros $14.00			G	S				
SAINTSBURY WINERY '88, Carneros, Reserve $20.00			S	S				
SEBASTIANI VINEYARDS '88, Sonoma Co., Reserve $10.00		S			B			
SEGHESIO WINERY '88, Sonoma Co., Reserve $12.00		S			S			
SELLARDS WINERY '88, Russian Riv., Graton Hills	S							B
SHAFER VINEYARDS '88, Napa $13.50			S		S			
CHARLES F. SHAW WINERY '88, Napa Vly. $10.50					B		B	
SIMI WINERY '88, Sonoma/Mendo/Napa $15.75	S		B					
ROBERT SINSKEY VINEYARDS '87, Napa Vly., Carneros				B				B

Chardonnay

2 AWARDS

San Diego	W. Coast Nat'l O.S.	State Fair	Dallas	San Fran	Farmers	Orange	L.A.	
S		B						**SONOMA CREEK WINERY** '88, Carneros $12.00
S				G				**ST. ANDREWS WINERY** '87, Napa Vly., Estate $13.25
					B	S		**ST. CLEMENT VINEYARDS** '88, Napa, Carneros, Abbotts Vnyd.
	B		B					**ST. FRANCIS WINERY** '88, Sonoma Vly., Estate $15.00
S		B						**ST. SUPERY VINEYARDS** '88, Napa Vly. $11.00
			S		B			**STAG'S LEAP WINE CELLARS** '88, Napa Vly. $18.00
B		B						**STERLING VINEYARDS** '88, Napa Vly. $14.50
			B		B			**STONE CREEK** '88, Alexander Vly. $9.00
					B	B		**M. G. VALLEJO WINERY** '89, California
	B	B						**VENTANA VINEYARDS** '88, Monterey, Crystal $16.00
B			B					**WEIBEL VINEYARDS** '88, Mendocino Co.
		G			S			**WENTE BROS.** '89, Central Coast $8.00
			B	B				**WENTE BROS.** '88, Central Coast, Reserve $12.00
B		B						**WILLIAM WHEELER WINERY** '88, Sonoma $12.00
		B		B				**WHITFORD CELLARS** '88, Napa Vly. $13.00
			B	B				**WILD HORSE WINERY** '88, San Luis Obispo Co. $13.00
B				B				**WINDSOR VINEYARDS** '88, Sonoma Co. $8.50
			B		G			**ZACA MESA WINERY** '88, Santa Barbara Reserve $16.50
		G			B			**ZACA MESA WINERY** '89, Santa Barbara Co. $11.00

Dry Creek Vineyard
1989 DRY CHENIN BLANC
CALIFORNIA
ALCOHOL 11.8% BY VOLUME

HACIENDA
1989 CLARKSBURG
Dry Chenin Blanc
RESIDUAL SUGAR 0.75 GRAMS/100 ML
PRODUCED AND BOTTLED BY HACIENDA WINERY
SONOMA, CALIFORNIA • B.W. 4623 • ALCOHOL 11.5% BY VOLUME

Chenin Blanc

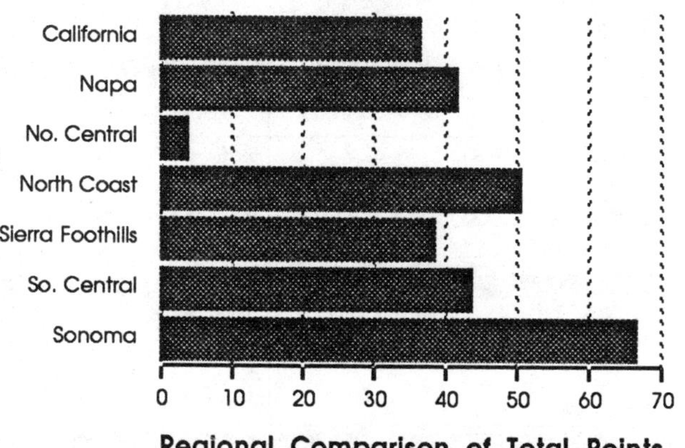

Regional Comparison of Total Points

(Gold=5   Silver=3   Bronze=1)

Highest   individual   wine   totals

2 0   **DRY CREEK VINEYARD**
'89, California, Dry $6.50

1 6   **HACIENDA WINERY**
'89, Clarksburg $6.50

1 5   **SIMI WINERY**
'89, Mendocino Co. $6.00

1 4   **ARCIERO WINERY**
'89, Paso Robles, Estate $4.50

1 2   **PARDUCCI WINE CELLARS**
'89, Mendocino Co. $4.50

1 2   **VILLA MT. EDEN WINERY**
'88, Napa Vly. $5.99

1 2   **WHITE OAK VINEYARDS**
'89, Alexander Vly. $6.75

1 0   **GRAND CRU VINEYARDS**
'89, Clarksburg, Premium $6.50

1 0   **WEIBEL VINEYARDS**
'89, Mendocino Co., Dry

1 0   **WINDSOR VINEYARDS**
'89, Alexander Vly. $6.00

Chenin Blanc

	L.A.	Orange	Farmers	San Fran	Dallas	State Fair	Nat'l O.S.	W. Coast	San Diego
6 AWARDS									
DRY CREEK VINEYARD '89, California, Dry $6.50		G	S		G	B	G		B
HACIENDA WINERY '89, Clarksburg $6.50	S	S	B	S	G	B			
WHITE OAK VINEYARDS '89, Alexander Vly. $6.75	S	B	B			S	S	B	
5 AWARDS									
HUSCH VINEYARDS '89, Mendocino, La Ribera $6.50		B	B	B				B	B
SIMI WINERY '89, Mendocino Co. $6.00	G	G	S	B					B
4 AWARDS									
ARCIERO WINERY '89, Paso Robles, Estate $4.50			G		B	G			S
DE MOOR WINERY '89, Napa Vly. $6.25	B	B	B					B	
FETZER VINEYARDS '88, California $5.99			S		B		S		B
GRAND CRU VINEYARDS '89, Clarksburg, Premium Sel. $6.50		B		S		B	G		
PARDUCCI WINE CELLARS '89, Mendocino Co. $4.50	S	S				B	G		
VILLA MT. EDEN WINERY '88, Napa Vly. $5.99		G			S	B	S		
WINDSOR VINEYARDS '89, Alexander Vly. $6.00		B	B	S			G		
3 AWARDS									
CALLAWAY VINEYARD '89, Temecula, Morning Harvest $6.50			S					B	B
GLEN ELLEN WINERY '89, California Proprietor's Reserve $4.50		B				S			B
MILAT VINEYARDS '89, Napa Vly. $6.50			S	B			G		
MOUNT PALOMAR WINERY '89, Temecula $6.00			B					B	B
PRESTON VINEYARDS '89, Dry Creek Vly., Estate $7.50		G				B			S

Chenin Blanc

3 AWARDS

San Diego	W. Coast	Nat'l O.S.	State Fair	Dallas	San Fran	Farmers	Orange	L.A.	Winery
S		B					G		**WHITEHALL LANE WINERY** '89, Napa Vly.

2 AWARDS

San Diego	W. Coast	Nat'l O.S.	State Fair	Dallas	San Fran	Farmers	Orange	L.A.	Winery
		B		B					**CALLAWAY VINEYARD** '88, Temecula, Morning Harvest
						B	S		**CILURZO VINEYARD** '89, Temecula $6.00
			S					G	**FETZER VINEYARDS** '89, California $5.99
		B		B					**FOLIE A DEUX WINERY** '89, Napa Vly.
			S				G		**GEYSER PEAK WINERY** '89, Alexander Vly. $5.95
	B							B	**GREENSTONE WINERY** '89, Amador Co.
						S		B	**BARON HERZOG WINE CELLARS** '89, California $4.99
G					B				**KENWOOD WINERY** '89, California $6.50
S				S					**MARTIN BROTHERS WINERY** '89, Paso Robles, Estate
						B	S		**NAPA RIDGE WINERY** '89, Central Coast $5.25
				B		S			**PARDUCCI WINE CELLARS** '88, Mendocino Co. $6.49
			S					B	**R. H. PHILLIPS VINEYARD** '89, Yolo Co., Dunnigan Hills Vnyd. $3.00
B		B							**SANTA BARBARA WINERY** '88, Santa Ynez Vly., Barrel Ferm.
			B	B					**SIMI WINERY** '88, Mendocino Co. $6.00
							G	G	**WEIBEL VINEYARDS** '89, Mendocino Co., Dry

DE LOACH
VINEYARDS
ESTATE BOTTLED
RUSSIAN RIVER VALLEY
GEWÜRZTRAMINER
1989 LATE HARVEST

1989
ST. FRANCIS
SONOMA COUNTY
GEWÜRZTRAMINER
PRODUCED AND BOTTLED BY
ST. FRANCIS WINERY
KENWOOD CALIFORNIA U.S.A.
ALC. 12.0% VOL
A KOBRAND CORPORATION
CALIFORNIA SELECTION

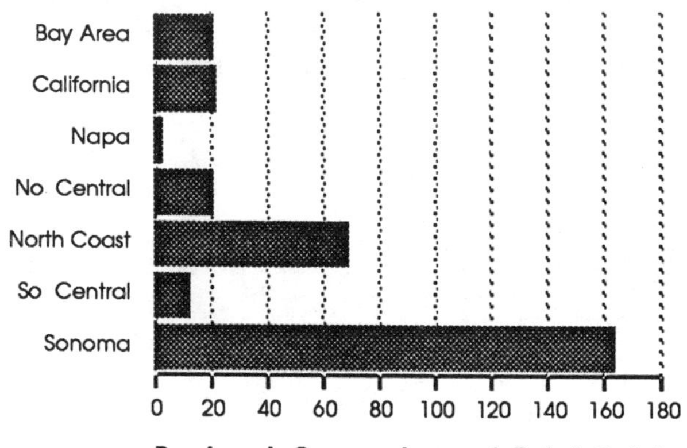

Regional Comparison of Total Points

(Gold=5   Silver=3   Bronze=1)

Highest individual wine totals

2 4   **DE LOACH VINEYARDS**
'89, Russian River, LH $12.00

2 1   **THOMAS FOGARTY WINERY**
'89, Spring Ridge Vnyd. $9.00

1 8   **THOMAS FOGARTY WINERY**
'89, Ventana Vnyd. $9.00

1 5   **ST. FRANCIS WINERY**
'89, Sonoma Co. $7.50

1 3   **FETZER VINEYARDS**
'89, California $5.99

1 2   **FIELD STONE WINERY**
'89, Alexander Vly. $7.75

1 2   **HUSCH VINEYARDS**
'89, Anderson Vly. $8.00

1 0   **HANDLEY CELLARS**
'89, Anderson Vly. $7.50

1 0   **QUAFF WINERY**
'89, Sonoma Co. $6.25

1 0   **WEIBEL VINEYARDS**
'89, Mendocino Co. $5.00

1 0   **WINDSOR VINEYARDS**
'87, Alexander Vly., LH $12.00

Gewurztraminer
0 - 3.0 Residual Sugar

	L.A.	Orange	Farmers	San Fran	Dallas	State Fair	Nat'l O.S.	W. Coast	San Diego
7 AWARDS									
NAVARRO VINEYARDS — '88, Anderson Vly. $8.50	S	B		B		B	B	B	B
6 AWARDS									
HUSCH VINEYARDS — '89, Anderson Vly., Estate $8.00	B	B	B			G		S	B
5 AWARDS									
BUENA VISTA WINERY — '87, Carneros, Estate	S				B		B	S	B
DAVIS BYNUM WINERY — '89, Russian River, McIlroy Vnyd. $8.00	B				B	S		S	B
FETZER VINEYARDS — '89, California $5.99	B	G				S	B		S
THOMAS FOGARTY WINERY — '89, Santa Cruz, Spring Ridge $9.00		G		S		G	S		G
ST. FRANCIS WINERY — '89, Sonoma Co. $7.50		G		B		B	S	G	
4 AWARDS									
FIELD STONE WINERY — '89, Alexander Vly. $7.75	S	S		S				S	
THOMAS FOGARTY WINERY — '89, Monterey, Ventana Vnyd. $9.00	G	G					G		S
GRAND CRU VINEYARDS — '89, Alexander Vly., Premium Sel. $9.00		B	B				B	B	
HANDLEY CELLARS — '89, Anderson Vly. $7.50		B		B		S			G
NAPA RIDGE WINERY — '89, Central Coast $5.25		B				B		B	B
NEVADA CITY WINERY — '89, Sonoma Co. $7.00				B		B		B	B
QUAFF WINERY — '89, Sonoma Co. $6.25	G	S				B			B
WEIBEL VINEYARDS — '89, Mendocino Co. $5.00		G		S				B	B
3 AWARDS									
BERINGER VINEYARDS — '89, North Coast $5.25				B				S	B
DE LOACH VINEYARDS — '89, Russian River Vly. $7.50				B	B			B	

Gewurztraminer
0 - 3.0 Residual Sugar

San Diego	W. Coast	Nat'l O.S.	State Fair	Dallas	San Fran	Farmers	Orange	L.A.	Wine
									3 AWARDS
					G		B	B	**FIRESTONE VINEYARD** '89, Santa Ynez Vly. $7.50
B			B				B		**BARON HERZOG WINE CELLARS** '89, Sonoma Co., Calif. Sel. $7.39
S	B						S		**Z. MOORE WINERY** '89, Russian River Vly. $8.50
									2 AWARDS
B							B		**CHATEAU ST. JEAN** '89, Sonoma Co. $8.00
S					B				**CLOS DU BOIS WINES** '89, Alexander Vly. $8.00
S						S			**DE LOACH VINEYARDS** '88, Russian River Vly. $7.50
G							S		**GEYSER PEAK WINERY** '89, California, Soft
		S		G					**GUNDLACH BUNDSCHU WINERY** '88, Sonoma, Rhinefarm Vnyd.
	S							B	**OBESTER WINERY** '89, Anderson Vly. $7.00
		S					G		**PARDUCCI WINE CELLARS** '88, Mendocino Co.

Gewurztraminer
3.1 + Residual Sugar

	L.A.	Orange Farmers	San Fran	Dallas	State Fair	Nat'l O.S.	W. Coast	San Diego
6 AWARDS								
DE LOACH VINEYARDS '89, Russian River, LH, R.S. 13.0 $12.00	G	S S	G		G			S
4 AWARDS								
WINDSOR VINEYARDS '87, Alexander Vly., LH, R.S. 5.6 $12.00	S	S B	S					
3 AWARDS								
CHATEAU ST. JEAN '86, Belle Terre Vnyds., SLH, R.S. 15.8 $14.00	S	B	B					
2 AWARDS								
CLOS DU BOIS WINES '89, Fleur D'Alexandra, LH, R.S. 7.0 $18.00	S				S			
HUSCH VINEYARDS '89, Anderson Vly., LH, R.S. 17.0 $12.00	G							B
Z. MOORE WINERY '89, Carneros, SLH, R.S. 10.0 $7.50		S					S	

J. Lohr
JOHANNISBERG RIESLING
Monterey County
LATE HARVEST
PRODUCED & BOTTLED BY J. LOHR WINERY
SAN JOSE, CALIFORNIA ALCOHOL 10.5% BY VOLUME

GEYSER PEAK
1989
CALIFORNIA
SOFT JOHANNISBERG RIESLING
A soft, delicate White Riesling
in the German Style.
PRODUCED AND BOTTLED BY GEYSER PEAK WINERY
GEYSERVILLE, CALIFORNIA U.S.A. ALC. 9.5% BY VOL.

Johannisberg Riesling

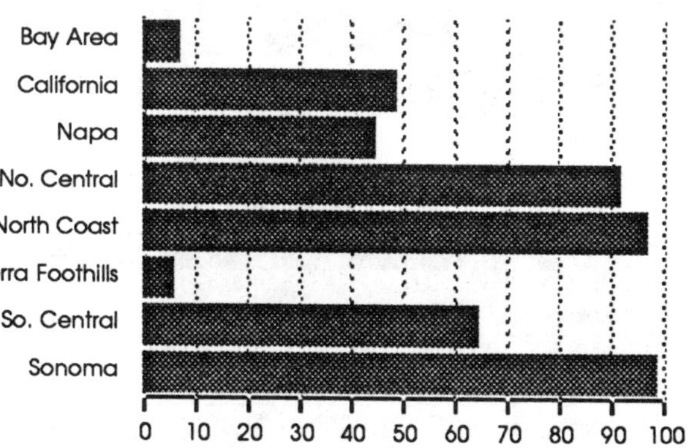

Regional Comparison of Total Points

(Gold=5   Silver=3   Bronze=1)

Highest individual wine totals

2 3
FETZER VINEYARDS
'89, California $6.50

2 2
FETZER VINEYARDS
'88, Sonoma, Reserve, LH $10.00

2 2
J. LOHR WINERY
'89, Monterey Co. LH $9.00

2 0
CHATEAU ST. JEAN
'88, Alexander Vly., SLH $20.00

1 9
GREENWOOD RIDGE VINEYARDS
'89, Mendocino, LH $18.00

1 8
GEYSER PEAK WINERY
'89, California, Soft $5.95

1 7
RODNEY STRONG VINEYARDS
'86, Le Baron Vnyd., LH $9.00

1 5
GREENWOOD RIDGE VINEYARDS
'89, Mendocino, Estate $8.00

1 5
KENDALL-JACKSON WINERY
'89, Clear Lake, Reserve $9.00

1 4
NAVARRO VINEYARDS
'86, Anderson Vly., LH $25.00

1 1
KENWOOD WINERY
'86, Sonoma Vly., LH $8.50

	L.A.	Orange	Farmers	San Fran	Dallas	State Fair	Nat'l O.S.	W. Coast	San Diego
FETZER VINEYARDS '89, California $6.50									
KENDALL-JACKSON WINERY '89, Clear Lake, Vintner's Reserve $9.00	S	B	S	S		B		S	B
6 AWARDS									
GEYSER PEAK WINERY '89, California, Soft $5.95	S	G				S	S	S	B
TREFETHEN VINEYARDS '89, Napa Vly., White, Estate $8.75		B	B		B	B		S	B
5 AWARDS									
GREENWOOD RIDGE VINEYARDS '89, Mendocino, Estate $8.00	G	B	S				G		B
4 AWARDS									
KONOCTI WINERY '89, Lake Co. $7.50		S				B		B	G
J. LOHR WINERY '89, Monterey, Greenfield Vnyds. $6.00		G				B		B	B
STORRS WINERY '89, Santa Cruz Mtns. $9.00		S		B	B				B
VENTANA VINEYARDS '88, Monterey $6.50	B	B		B	B				
3 AWARDS									
BALLARD CANYON WINERY '89, Santa Ynez Vly., Estate	S	S							B
CLOS DU MURIEL '89, Temecula $6.99	B		S		B				
FIRESTONE VINEYARD '89, Santa Ynez Vly. $7.50		B			B				S
GAINEY VINEYARD '89, Santa Barbara Co. $7.75	G		B						B
HAGAFEN CELLARS '89, Napa Vly. $8.75		G		S			B		
WILLIAM HILL WINERY '89, Willamette Vly. $7.50		B						G	B
PAUL MASSON VINEYARDS '88, Monterey Co., Arroyo Seco		B			B				B
OBESTER WINERY '89, Monterey, Ventana Vnyd. $7.00				B				S	B

Johannisberg Riesling
0 - 3.0 Residual Sugar

San Diego	W. Coast	Nat'l O.S.	State Fair	Dallas	San Fran	Farmers	Orange	L.A.	
									3 AWARDS
G			B			B			**V. SATTUI WINERY** '89, Napa Vly., Dry $8.50
B	B					S			**V. SATTUI WINERY** '89, Napa Vly., Off Dry $8.50
			S				B	S	**VENTANA VINEYARDS** '89, Monterey, Dry $6.50
									2 AWARDS
		S				B			**BAILY VINEYARD** '89, Temecula, Mother's Vnyd. $7.50
			B				B		**BRICELAND VINEYARDS** '89, Anderson Vly., Dennison $9.00
							B	G	**BUENA VISTA WINERY** '88, Carneros
			B					S	**CHATEAU ST. JEAN** '89, Sonoma Co. $9.00
						B		G	**JEKEL VINEYARDS** '88, Arroyo Seco, Dry Style $7.50
			S				B		**MARK WEST VINEYARDS** '87, Russian River Vly., Estate $7.50
S					B				**PARDUCCI WINE CELLARS** '89, Mendocino Co. $6.50
			B			B			**RENAISSANCE VINEYARD** '88, North Yuba $8.00
						S		B	**SANTA BARBARA WINERY** '88, Santa Ynez, Paradis Dry $7.50

	L.A.	Orange	Farmers	San Fran	Dallas	State Fair	Nat'l O.S.	W. Coast	San Diego
8 AWARDS									
J. LOHR WINERY '89, Monterey Co. LH, R.S. 10.3 $9.00	G	S	B	B	S		S	S	S
7 AWARDS									
GREENWOOD RIDGE VINEYARDS '89, Mendocino, LH, R.S. 21.4 $18.00	G	S	B	B		G	S		B
6 AWARDS									
CHATEAU ST. JEAN '88, Alexander Vly., SLH, $20.00	G	S	S	B	S				G
FETZER VINEYARDS '88, Sonoma, Reserve, LH, R.S. 21.0 $10.00	G	B	G	B		G		G	
5 AWARDS									
BARON HERZOG WINE CELLARS '89, California, LH, R.S. 19.7 $7.43	B	S	B			B	S		
RODNEY STRONG VINEYARDS '86, Le Baron Vnyd., LH, R.S. 14.1 $9.00	G		B	G			S	S	
WINDSOR VINEYARDS '88, Sonoma Co., LH, R.S. 6.4 $12.00	G		B	B			B	B	
4 AWARDS									
NAVARRO VINEYARDS '86, Anderson Vly., LH, R.S. 25.4 $25.00			G	S			S		S
WENTE BROS. '87, Arroyo Seco, Reserve, R.S. 9.8 $10.00	S			B			G		B
3 AWARDS									
JEKEL VINEYARDS '88, Arroyo Seco, LH, R.S. 14.0 $12.00	S					B	S		
KENWOOD WINERY '86, Sonoma Vly., Estate, LH, R.S. 22.8 $8.50		S		S	G				
2 AWARDS									
FREEMARK ABBEY WINERY '89, Edelwein Gold, LH, R.S. 21.7 $22.00		S							B
KENDALL-JACKSON WINERY '85, Lake Co., SLH, R.S. 16.3 $15.00	S						G		
KONOCTI WINERY '86, Lake Co., LH, R.S. 13.2 $10.00				B			B		
MOUNT PALOMAR WINERY '89, Temecula,	S						S		
VENTANA VINEYARDS '87, Monterey, LH, R.S. 15.0 $10.00				S		S			

1987
BENZIGER
A TRIBUTE

COSENTINO
S E L E C T
1987
"THE POET"
PREMIER RED
MERITAGE
M. Cosentino
A CALIFORNIA TABLE WINE
A FINE TABLE WINE VINTED AND BOTTLED BY
COSENTINO VINTNERS ST. HELENA, CA FOR
M. COSENTINO YOUNTVILLE, NAPA VALLEY

Meritage Red

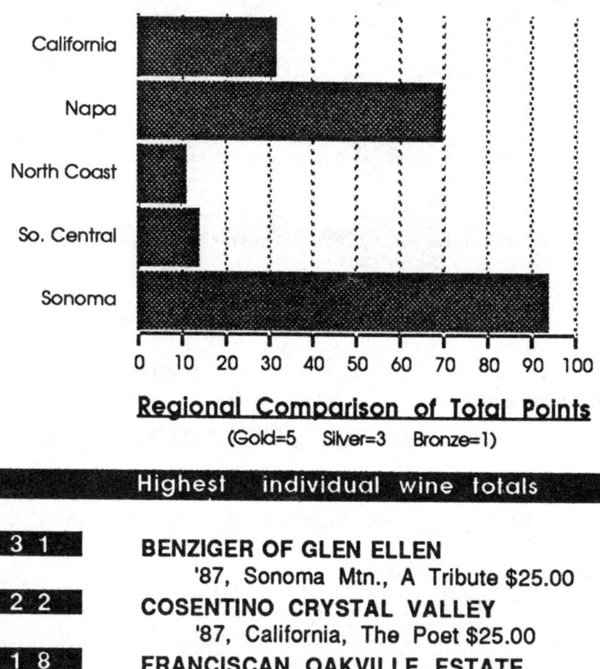

Regional Comparison of Total Points

(Gold=5   Silver=3   Bronze=1)

Highest individual wine totals

31 BENZIGER OF GLEN ELLEN
'87, Sonoma Mtn., A Tribute $25.00

22 COSENTINO CRYSTAL VALLEY
'87, California, The Poet $25.00

18 FRANCISCAN OAKVILLE ESTATE
'86, Napa, Red Table Wine $16.00

15 CLOS DU BOIS WINES
'86, Alexander Vly., Marlstone $19.00

12 DRY CREEK VINEYARD
'86, Dry Creek Vly., Blende $22.00

11 INGLENOOK NAPA VALLEY
'85, Napa., Reunion $35.00

11 LYETH WINERY
'86, Alexander Vly. $22.50

10 GUENOC WINERY
'87, Langtry, Lake/Napa $35.00

9 JUSTIN VINEYARDS
'87, Paso Robles, Reserve $15.00

Meritage Red

	L.A.	Orange Farmers		San Fran	Dallas	State Fair	Nat'l O.S.	W. Coast	San Diego
9 AWARDS									
BENZIGER OF GLEN ELLEN '87, Sonoma Mtn., A Tribute $25.00	B	B	G	B	G	S	G	G	G
7 AWARDS									
CLOS DU BOIS WINES '86, Alexander Vly., Marlstone $19.00		B	S	B	B	G	S	B	
6 AWARDS									
COSENTINO CRYSTAL VALLEY '87, California, The Poet $25.00	G	G	S	G				S	B
DRY CREEK VINEYARD '86, Dry Creek Vly., Blende $22.00	S	S	S		B		B	B	
FRANCISCAN OAKVILLE ESTATE '86, Napa Vly. Red Table Wine $16.00	S	S	G	G		B		B	
4 AWARDS									
GEYSER PEAK WINERY '86, Alexander Vly., Reserve $18.95						S	B	B	B
3 AWARDS									
CAIN CELLARS '86, Napa, Cain Five $30.00				S		B			B
INGLENOOK NAPA VALLEY '85, Napa., Reunion $35.00	G	G		B					
JUSTIN VINEYARDS '87, Paso Robles, Reserve $15.00	G	B		S					
LYETH WINERY '86, Alexander Vly. $22.50		G		S					S
STERLING VINEYARDS '86, Napa Vly., Reserve $45.00		S			B	S			
STERLING VINEYARDS '86, Napa Vly., Three Palms Red	B	S			B				
2 AWARDS									
GUENOC WINERY '87, Langtry, Lake Co./Napa Co. $35.00		G				G			
INGLENOOK NAPA VALLEY '86, Napa Vly., Reunion $35.00			B				G		
KONOCTI WINERY '87, Lake Co., Estate Reserve $17.00		B							B
MERRYVALE VINEYARDS '86, Napa Vly.	S							B	

Meritage Red

San Diego	W. Coast	Nat'l O.S.	State Fair	Dallas	San Fran	Farmers	Orange	L.A.	
									2 AWARDS
			S		S				**PARDUCCI WINE CELLARS** '86, Mendocino Co., Cabernet/Merlot

Meritage
is a Reserve~Quality
bottling made in the Bordeaux style
88% Sauvignon Blanc 12% Semillon
Clear Lake White Table Wine
1988 Estate Bottled
Produced & Bottled by
KONOCTI
Winery, Kelseyville, California, U.S.A. 95451
Alc. 12.8% by Vol.

Inglenook.
NAPA · VALLEY
ESTATE BOTTLED
1988
Gravion
NAPA VALLEY SAUVIGNON BLANC
51%
NAPA VALLEY SEMILLON
49%

Meritage White

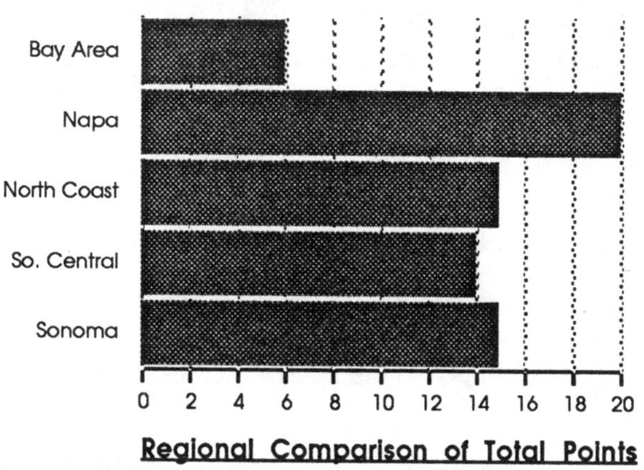

Regional Comparison of Total Points
(Gold=5   Silver=3   Bronze=1)

Highest individual wine totals

1 5 KONOCTI WINERY
'88, Clear Lake, Meritage $14.00

1 4 INGLENOOK NAPA VALLEY
'88, Napa Vly., Gravion $9.50

8 BENZIGER OF GLEN ELLEN
'88, Sonoma, Estate $15.00

7 DE LORIMER WINERY
'88, Alexander Vly., Spectrum $8.50

6 BAILY VINEYARD
'89, Temecula, Montage $10.00

6 CONCANNON VINEYARD
'87, Livermore, Assemblage

5 CARMENET
'87, Edna Vly.

<table>
<thead>
<tr><th>Meritage White</th><th>L.A.</th><th>Orange</th><th>Farmers</th><th>San Fran</th><th>Dallas</th><th>State Fair</th><th>Nat'l O.S.</th><th>W. Coast</th><th>San Diego</th></tr>
</thead>
<tbody>
<tr><td colspan="10">7 AWARDS</td></tr>
<tr><td>KONOCTI WINERY
'88, Clear Lake, Meritage, Estate $14.00</td><td>S</td><td>S</td><td>S</td><td>B</td><td></td><td>B</td><td></td><td>S</td><td>B</td></tr>
<tr><td colspan="10">4 AWARDS</td></tr>
<tr><td>BAILY VINEYARD
'89, Temecula, Montage $10.00</td><td></td><td></td><td>B</td><td>S</td><td></td><td>B</td><td></td><td></td><td>B</td></tr>
<tr><td>BENZIGER OF GLEN ELLEN
'88, Sonoma, Estate $15.00</td><td></td><td></td><td>S</td><td>B</td><td>S</td><td></td><td></td><td>B</td><td></td></tr>
<tr><td>INGLENOOK NAPA VALLEY
'88, Napa Vly., Gravion $9.50</td><td>G</td><td>G</td><td>B</td><td></td><td></td><td></td><td></td><td>S</td><td></td></tr>
<tr><td colspan="10">3 AWARDS</td></tr>
<tr><td>DE LORIMER WINERY
'88, Alexander Vly., Estate, Spectrum $8.50</td><td></td><td></td><td>G</td><td>B</td><td></td><td>B</td><td></td><td></td><td></td></tr>
<tr><td colspan="10">2 AWARDS</td></tr>
<tr><td>CONCANNON VINEYARD
'87, Livermore Vly., Assemblage</td><td></td><td></td><td>B</td><td></td><td></td><td></td><td></td><td></td><td>G</td></tr>
<tr><td>VICHON WINERY
'88, Napa Vly. $9.50</td><td></td><td></td><td></td><td>B</td><td></td><td></td><td></td><td>B</td><td></td></tr>
</tbody>
</table>

ESTATE BOTTLED

O F G L E N E L L E N

1987

SONOMA VALLEY

MERLOT

ALCOHOL 12.8% BY VOLUME

1987

MARKHAM.

NAPA VALLEY

Merlot

MADE AND BOTTLED BY
MARKHAM VINEYARDS, ST. HELENA, CALIFORNIA, U.S.A.
ALCOHOL 13.5% BY VOLUME
CONTAINS SULFITES

Merlot

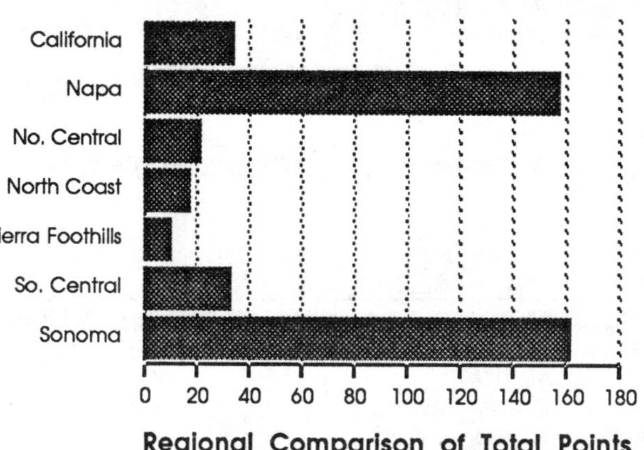

Highest   individual   wine   totals

2 3
BENZIGER OF GLEN ELLEN
'87, Sonoma Vly., Estate $15.00

2 0
MARKHAM VINEYARDS
'87, Napa Vly. $13.50

1 7
BRAREN PAULI WINERY
'87, Mauritson Vnyd. $12.50

1 3
CLOS DU BOIS WINES
'87, Sonoma Co. $12.00

1 2
CHRISTIAN BROTHERS
'86, Napa Vly. $8.50

1 2
COSENTINO CRYSTAL VALLEY
'88, California $17.00

1 1
GUENOC WINERY
'86, Napa Co./Lake Co. $12.00

1 1
GUNDLACH BUNDSCHU WINERY
'87, Rhinefarm Vnyds. $12.00

1 1
ST. CLEMENT VINEYARDS
'86, Napa Vly. $15.00

1 0
FRANCISCAN OAKVILLE ESTATE
'87, Napa Vly. $12.50

1 0
PAUL MASSON VINEYARDS
'87, Monterey Co. $8.00

Merlot

	L.A.	Orange	Farmers	San Fran	Dallas	State Fair	Nat'l O.S.	W. Coast	San Diego
8 AWARDS									
MARKHAM VINEYARDS '87, Napa Vly. $13.50	B	G	S		B	B	G	B	S
7 AWARDS									
BENZIGER OF GLEN ELLEN '87, Sonoma Vly., Estate $15.00	G	B		B		S	G	S	G
CLOS DU BOIS WINES '87, Sonoma Co. $12.00	B		S	B	S	B		S	B
6 AWARDS									
COSENTINO CRYSTAL VALLEY '88, California $17.00	S	S	B	B		B			S
INGLENOOK NAPA VALLEY '86, Napa Vly., Reserve $11.25		B	B	B		B	B	B	
5 AWARDS									
BRAREN PAULI WINERY '87, Alexander Vly., Mauritson Vnyd. $12.50		G		S	G		B	S	
GUENOC WINERY '86, Napa Co./Lake Co. $12.00		B			S		B	S	S
GUNDLACH BUNDSCHU WINERY '87, Sonoma, Rhinefarm Vnyds. $12.00	S		S		B	S			B
KENDALL-JACKSON WINERY '87, Sonoma Co., Proprietor's $20.00		S		S		G		S	B
RABBIT RIDGE VINEYARDS '87, Sonoma Co., Clairvaux Vnyd. $12.00		B	S				G	S	B
ST. CLEMENT VINEYARDS '86, Napa Vly. $15.00			B	S	S			S	B
WILD HORSE WINERY '88, Central Coast $13.00			B	S		B		B	B
WINDSOR VINEYARDS '86, Russian River Vly. $10.00			B			S	B	B	B
4 AWARDS									
CHRISTIAN BROTHERS '86, Napa Vly. $8.50		S				B	S	G	
FRANCISCAN OAKVILLE ESTATE '87, Napa Vly. $12.50			B	S	S	S			
GOLDEN CREEK VINEYARD '88, Sonoma Co. $12.00				B	B			B	B
PAUL MASSON VINEYARDS '87, Monterey Co. $8.00		G		B	S		B		

Merlot

San Diego	W. Coast	Nat'l O.S.	State Fair	Dallas	San Fran	Farmers	Orange	L.A.	Wine
									4 AWARDS
	B		B		B				**VICHON WINERY** '88, Napa Vly. $16.00
									3 AWARDS
	B	S				G			**BERGFIELD CELLARS** '87, Napa Vly. $12.00
				B		B	S		**CLOS DU VAL WINE CO.** '87, Napa Vly., Stags Leap $17.00
		G					S		**CONN CREEK WINERY** '87, Napa Vly., Collins Vnyd.
			S	B					**FENESTRA CELLARS** '88, Central Coast $12.50
	S				B		B		**GLEN ELLEN WINERY** '87, California, Proprietor's Reserve $6.00
			S		B		B		**LAMBERT BRIDGE** '88, Sonoma $16.00
	S					G			**LOUIS M. MARTINI** '87, Russian River, Los Vinedos Del Rio
	B	S				G			**NAPA CREEK WINERY** '87, Napa Vly.
	S				B	G			**RICHARDSON VINEYARDS** '88, Sonoma, Carneros, Gregory $14.00
			B	S	B				**ROUND HILL CELLARS** '87, Napa Reserve $8.99
				B	B				**VICHON WINERY** '87, Napa Vly. $16.00
			B	B			G		**YORK MOUNTAIN WINERY** '87, San Luis Obispo $16.00
									2 AWARDS
	S				S				**BEL ARBORS** 'NV, American $6.00
	B		G						**BENZIGER OF GLEN ELLEN** '86, Sonoma Co.
				G					**BOEGER WINERY** '87, El Dorado, Estate $12.50
			B		B				**BOGLE VINEYARDS** '89, California $7.50
				S					**BUENA VISTA WINERY** '87, Carneros, Estate Reserve $16.50

Merlot

2 AWARDS

	L.A.	Orange	Farmers	San Fran	Dallas	State Fair	Nat'l O.S.	W. Coast	San Diego
CHATEAU SOUVERAIN '87, Sonoma Co.		S							B
MADRONA VINEYARDS '85, El Dorado, Estate $10.00				B		B			
LOUIS M. MARTINI '87, North Coast		S					S		
MILL CREEK VINEYARDS '86, Dry Creek Vly., Estate $9.00				B				S	
NEVADA CITY WINERY '87, Sierra Foothills		B							B
NEWTON VINEYARD '86, Napa Vly. $15.85			B				B		
NEWTON VINEYARD '87, Napa Vly. $16.75				S		B			
PARDUCCI WINE CELLARS '87, North Coast $9.50	S			S					
ROSENBLUM CELLARS '88, Napa Vly.		B						B	
SEBASTIANI VINEYARDS '88, Sonoma Co. $7.00		S				B			
SHAFER VINEYARDS '88, Napa $16.50	S			B					
SOLARI ESTATE '87, Napa, Dutch Henry Vnyd. $11.00	B					B			
ST. FRANCIS WINERY '87, Sonoma Vly., Estate $18.00				S		B			
STONEGATE WINERY '86, Napa, Estate $15.00		S		B					
STRAUS VINEYARDS '88, Napa Vly.		B							B
SWANSON WINERY '88, Napa Vly $15.00					B	S			
VENDANGE '89, California	B	S							

1986
CALIFORNIA
Petite Sirah

PRODUCED AND BOTTLED BY WINDSOR VINEYARDS, WINDSOR, SONOMA COUNTY, CALIFORNIA
ALCOHOL 13% BY VOLUME · CONTAINS SULFITES

Guenoc

1987
Guenoc Valley
Petite Sirah

PRODUCED AND BOTTLED BY GUENOC WINERY
MIDDLETOWN, CALIFORNIA, ALCOHOL 13% BY VOLUME

Petite Sirah

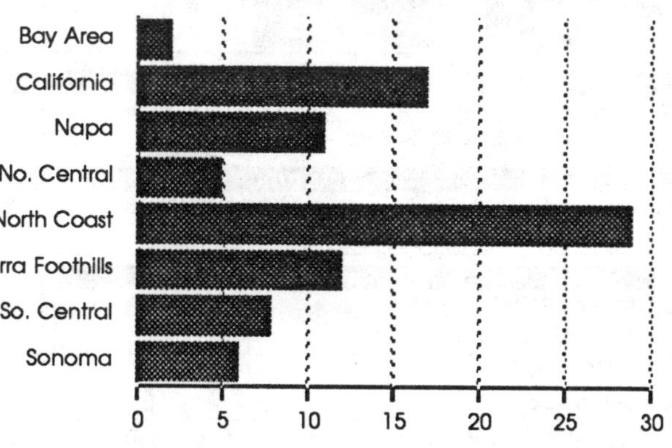

Regional Comparison of Total Points

(Gold=5   Silver=3   Bronze=1)

Highest   individual   wine   totals

1 7 **WINDSOR VINEYARDS**
'86, California $7.00

1 1 **GUENOC WINERY**
'87, Guenoc Vly. $9.00

1 0 **GUENOC WINERY**
'86, Lake Co.

7 **GRANITE SPRINGS WINERY**
'87, El Dorado, Granite Hill $8.50

6 **GLEN ELLEN WINERY**
'87, Paso Robles, Imagery $14.00

6 **PARDUCCI WINE CELLARS**
'86, Mendocino Co. $6.50

5 **VINCENT ARROYO WINERY**
'87, Napa Vly., Estate $9.00

5 **FOPPIANO WINE COMPANY**
'88, Sonoma Co. $9.50

5 **MIRASSOU VINEYARDS**
'87, Monterey, Family Sel. $7.00

5 **NEVADA COUNTY WINE GUILD**
'88, Sierra Foothills

	L.A.	Orange	Farmers	San Fran	Dallas	State Fair	Nat'l O.S.	W. Coast	San Diego
7 AWARDS									
WINDSOR VINEYARDS '86, California $7.00	S	S	B	S		B	G		B
5 AWARDS									
GUENOC WINERY '87, Guenoc Vly. $9.00			B	B		S		S	S
3 AWARDS									
VINCENT ARROYO WINERY '87, Napa Vly., Estate $9.00		B		S			B		
FOPPIANO WINE COMPANY '88, Sonoma Co. $9.50	S	B				B			
GRANITE SPRINGS WINERY '87, El Dorado, Granite Hill $8.50		B		B					G
MIRASSOU VINEYARDS '87, Monterey Co., Family Sel. $7.00		B	B						S
2 AWARDS									
GLEN ELLEN WINERY '87, Paso Robles, Imagery Series $14.00	B					G			
GUENOC WINERY '86, Lake Co.					G		G		
PARDUCCI WINE CELLARS '86, Mendocino Co. $6.50				G			B		
ROSENBLUM CELLARS '88, Napa Vly. $9.95			S						B

1987

DEHLINGER

Pinot Noir

RUSSIAN RIVER VALLEY
ESTATE BOTTLED

This intense, complex wine is selected from the steeper red hilltop areas with thinner soils in our eight acres of Pinot Noir. Produced and Bottled by Dehlinger Winery, Sebastopol, CA. CONTAINS SULFITES. Alc. 13.8% by vol.

Pinot Noir

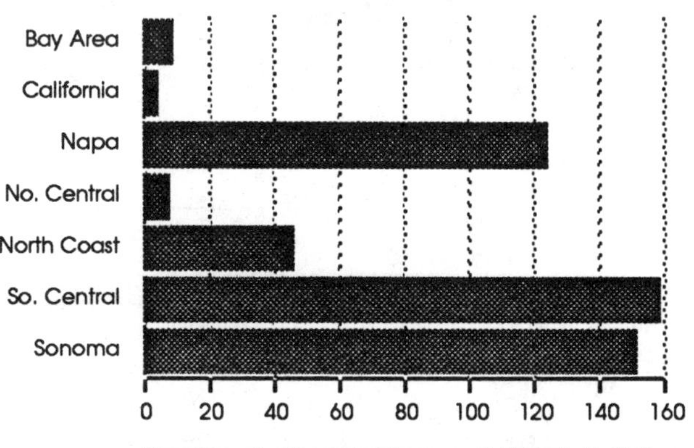

Regional Comparison of Total Points

(Gold=5   Silver=3   Bronze=1)

Highest   individual   wine   totals

2 7 **DEHLINGER WINERY**
'87, Russian River Vly. $14.00

2 6 **CAMBRIA WINERY**
'88, Julia's Vnyd. $16.00

2 5 **GARY FARRELL WINES**
'88, Russian Riv., Allen Vnyd. $25.00

1 7 **DAVIS BYNUM WINERY**
'87, Russian River Vly. $16.00

1 7 **THOMAS FOGARTY WINERY**
'87, Napa Vly., Carneros $15.00

1 7 **WILD HORSE WINERY**
'88, Santa Barbara Co. $13.00

1 5 **FETZER VINEYARDS**
'86, Mendocino, Reserve $17.50

1 3 **BEAULIEU VINEYARD**
'88, Carneros, Reserve $9.50

1 3 **RODNEY STRONG VINEYARDS**
'85, River East Vnyd. $10.00

1 2 **BOUCHAINE VINEYARDS**
'87, Napa Vly., Carneros $15.00

1 2 **GARY FARRELL WINES**
'88, Russian River Vly. $16.00

1 2 **STERLING VINEYARDS**
'87, Carneros, Winery Lake $16.00

Pinot Noir

	L.A.	Orange	Farmers	San Fran	Dallas	State Fair	Nat'l O.S.	W. Coast	San Diego
7 AWARDS									
DEHLINGER WINERY '87, Russian River Vly., Estate $14.00	G		S	S	G	B		G	G
GARY FARRELL WINES '88, Russian River Vly., Allen Vnyd. $25.00	G	G	B		G	G	B		S
WILD HORSE WINERY '88, Santa Barbara Co. $13.00	B	B	B			S	G	S	S
6 AWARDS									
CAMBRIA WINERY '88, Santa Maria Vly., Julia's Vnyd. $16.00	G	G	S			G		S	G
FETZER VINEYARDS '86, Mendocino Co., Reserve $17.50	G		S	B			B	G	G
5 AWARDS									
BEAULIEU VINEYARD '88, Napa Vly., Carneros Reserve $9.50		B	S		S	B			G
DAVIS BYNUM WINERY '87, Russian River Vly. $16.00		S	B	S	G		G		
THOMAS FOGARTY WINERY '87, Napa Vly., Carneros $15.00	G	S		B		S			G
GUNDLACH BUNDSCHU WINERY '88, Sonoma, Rhinefarm Vnyd. $12.00	B	B		B		S	S		
RODNEY STRONG VINEYARDS '85, River East Vnyd., Estate $10.00			S	S	B		G		B
4 AWARDS									
BOUCHAINE VINEYARDS '87, Napa Vly., Carneros $15.00			B	S			G		S
CASTORO CELLARS '88, Santa Barbara $9.50	B	G				B			B
GARY FARRELL WINES '88, Russian River Vly. $16.00		G	B					G	B
KENDALL-JACKSON WINERY '88, Santa Maria, Julia's Vnyd. $15.00	G					G		S	B
NAVARRO VINEYARDS '87, Anderson Vly., Reserve $14.00			B	B				G	S
CHARLES F. SHAW WINERY '87, Napa Vly., Carneros $14.50				B	B	B			S
STERLING VINEYARDS '87, Carneros, Winery Lake $16.00			S		S	S			S

Pinot Noir

San Diego	W. Coast Nat'l O.S.	State Fair	Dallas	San Fran	Farmers	Orange	L.A.	
3 AWARDS								
		S				S	B	**BABCOCK VINEYARDS** '88, Santa Barbara Co. $12.00
B				B	S			**BYRON VINEYARD** '87, Santa Barbara, Reserve $16.00
	G		B		B			**CLOS DU BOIS WINES** '87, Sonoma Co. $11.99
	S	B	S					**CORBETT CANYON VINEYARDS** '88, Central Coast, Reserve $8.25
B			S		B			**HUSCH VINEYARDS** '87, Anderson Vly. $13.00
	S		B			S		**TOBIN JAMES WINERY** '88, Monterey, Le Jus De Soleil
S	S	G						**PARDUCCI WINE CELLARS** '87, Mendocino Co. $12.00
S						G	S	**ZACA MESA WINERY** '88, Santa Barbara, Reserve
2 AWARDS								
	S					S		**AUSTIN CELLARS** '88, Santa Barbara Co.
		B				S		**BARGETTO WINERY** '87, Sierra Madre/Bien Nacido $16.00
				B		G		**BOUCHAINE VINEYARDS** '87, Napa Vly., Carneros, Reserve $19.00
S	S							**BUENA VISTA WINERY** '87, Carneros, Estate Reserve
	S	S						**J. CAREY CELLARS** '87, Santa Ynez Vly. $10.00
	S			B				**CONGRESS SPRINGS VINEYARDS** '88, Santa Clara Co. $10.00
					B	S		**CORBETT CANYON VINEYARDS** '88, Central Coast, Estate $15.00
		B				G		**CRESTON MANOR VINEYARD** '89, Paso Robles, Petit D'Noir $9.00
B						B		**M. MARION & COMPANY** '88, California
	G			B				**MARK WEST VINEYARDS** '86, Russian River Vly., Ellis Vnyd. $14.00

Pinot Noir

2 AWARDS

	L.A.	Orange	Farmers	San Fran	Dallas	State Fair	Nat'l O.S.	W. Coast	San Diego
ROBERT MONDAVI WINERY '87, Napa Vly., Reserve					G				G
ROBERT MONDAVI WINERY '88, Napa Vly.					G				B
NEVADA CITY WINERY '88, Nevada Co. $8.00						B			B
NEWLAN VINEYARDS '87, Napa Vly., Estate	B	S							
RICHARDSON VINEYARDS '88, Sonoma Vly., Carneros, Sangiacomo		B						S	
ROCHE WINERY '88, Carneros					B				B
SAINTSBURY WINERY '88, Carneros $15.00				S	S				
SANFORD WINERY '87, Santa Barbara Co. $14.50					S	B			
SANTA BARBARA WINERY '88, Santa Ynez Vly.		G						S	
SANTA BARBARA WINERY '88, Santa Ynez Vly., Reserve $20.00				B		B			
SEA RIDGE WINERY '88, Sonoma Coast $11.75			B						S
SEGHESIO WINERY '87, Russian River, Reserve $12.00				S					B
SEGHESIO WINERY '87, Russian River Vly.		B							B
ROBERT SINSKEY VINEYARDS '88, Napa Vly., Carneros, Estate $18.00		B		S					
WEIBEL VINEYARDS '88, Mendocino Co. $5.49		B				S			
WESTWOOD WINERY '87, Napa Vly., Haynes Vnyd., Reserve $15.00				G		S			
WINDSOR VINEYARDS '86, Los Carneros $10.00			B					S	

GREENWOOD
RIDGE
VINEYARDS

ANDERSON VALLEY
SAUVIGNON BLANC
1989

ALCOHOL 12.5% BY VOLUME

Konocti

Fumé Blanc

Lake County

Sauvignon Blanc

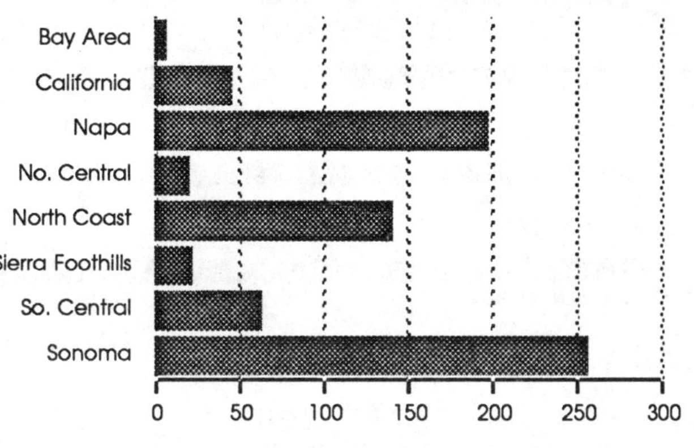

Regional Comparison of Total Points

(Gold=5   Silver=3   Bronze=1)

Highest individual wine totals

2 3   **GREENWOOD RIDGE VINEYARDS**
'89, Anderson Vly. $7.50

2 0   **GRGICH HILLS CELLAR**
'88, Napa Vly., Fume $10.00

1 9   **KONOCTI WINERY**
'89, Lake Co. $7.50

1 8   **CHALK HILL WINERY**
'85, Chalk Hill, LH $10.00

1 6   **MARKHAM VINEYARDS**
'89, Napa Vly. $7.00

1 3   **BUENA VISTA WINERY**
'89, Lake Co. $8.50

1 3   **PARDUCCI WINE CELLARS**
'88, North Coast $7.49

1 2   **GRAND CRU VINEYARDS**
'88, Sonoma, Premium $9.00

1 2   **KENDALL-JACKSON WINERY**
'89, Clear Lake, Vintner's $9.00

1 1   **DE LOACH VINEYARDS**
'89, Russian River, Fume $9.00

1 1   **HANDLEY CELLARS**
'88, Dry Creek Vly. $8.00

1 1   **VENTANA VINEYARDS**
'89, Monterey $8.00

Sauvignon Blanc

	L.A.	Orange	Farmers	San Fran	Dallas	State Fair	Nat'l O.S.	W. Coast	San Diego
8 AWARDS									
GRGICH HILLS CELLAR '88, Napa Vly., Fume $10.00	G	S	B	B	B	S	S		S
6 AWARDS									
MARKHAM VINEYARDS '89, Napa Vly. $7.00		S	S	B		B		G	S
5 AWARDS									
BUENA VISTA WINERY '89, Lake Co. $8.50	B		G			S		S	B
GREENWOOD RIDGE VINEYARDS '89, Anderson Vly. $7.50	S	G	G					G	G
HANDLEY CELLARS '88, Dry Creek Vly. $8.00			S		S	B	S		B
KONOCTI WINERY '89, Lake Co. $7.50	S	G		B		G		G	
PARDUCCI WINE CELLARS '88, North Coast $7.49	B	S	S	S			S		
WILLIAM WHEELER WINERY '88, Dry Creek Vly. $8.00		S		B	B	B			S
4 AWARDS									
AUDUBON CELLARS '88, Napa Vly., Pope Vnyd. $8.25		B				G		S	B
BEAULIEU VINEYARD '88, Napa Vly, Estate		B					B	G	B
BENZIGER OF GLEN ELLEN '88, Sonoma Co.		S			B			S	B
CHALK HILL WINERY '85, Chalk Hill, LH $10.00		G	G	S	G				
DRY CREEK VINEYARD '89, Sonoma Co., Fume $9.25		S				S		S	B
GRAND CRU VINEYARDS '88, Sonoma Co., Premium Sel. $9.00		G	B	S		S			
JEPSON VINEYARDS '88, Mendocino Co. $7.50		B		B	B	B			
KENDALL-JACKSON WINERY '89, Clear Lake, Vintner's Reserve $9.00	G			S		S		B	
MURPHY-GOODE WINERY '88, Alexander Vly. $8.50		B		G				S	B

San Diego	W. Coast	Nat'l O.S.	State Fair	Dallas	San Fran	Farmers	Orange	L.A.	
									4 AWARDS
S			B	B		B			**PRESTON VINEYARDS** '89, Dry Creek Vly., Reserve $10.00
B	B		B			B			**CHARLES F. SHAW WINERY** '89, Napa Vly. $9.50
B			B			G	B		**SIMI WINERY** '88, Sonoma Co. $8.50
	B		B				G	B	**ST. CLEMENT VINEYARDS** '89, Napa Vly. $9.75
	B	B	B	B					**ST. SUPERY VINEYARDS** '88, Napa Vly., Dollarhide Ranch $7.50
									3 AWARDS
S			B					B	**ARCIERO WINERY** '89, Paso Robles $7.49
G	B		B						**BALVERNE WINERY** '88, Chalk Hill, Stonecrest Vnyd. $6.50
	G						B	B	**BYRON VINEYARD** '89, Santa Barbara
B	B		S						**J. CAREY CELLARS** '88, Santa Ynez Vly. $9.00
			S			B	G		**CHATEAU ST. JEAN** '88, La Petite Etoile Vnyd. $10.50
B			B			G			**CLOS PEGASE WINERY** '87, Napa Vly., Fume $9.50
G			B			G			**DE LOACH VINEYARDS** '89, Russian River Vly., Fume $9.00
S	B	G							**DOMAINE NAPA WINERY** '88, Napa Vly., Michael A. Penet
			S		B		B		**DOMAINE NAPA WINERY** '89, Napa Vly. $8.50
G			B		B				**GARY FARRELL WINES** '88, Russian River Vly. $8.75
					B	B	B		**FENESTRA CELLARS** '88, Livermore Vly. $8.50
			B	S		G			**FRITZ CELLARS** '88, Dry Creek Vly. $7.99
G				B		G			**KENDALL-JACKSON WINERY** '88, Lake Co., Vintner's Reserve $9.00

Sauvignon Blanc

	L.A.	Orange	Farmers	San Fran	Dallas	State Fair	Nat'l O.S.	W. Coast	San Diego
3 AWARDS									
LOUIS M. MARTINI '89, Napa Vly. $6.99			G					B	B
PRESTON VINEYARDS '89, Dry Creek, Cuvee De Fume $8.00			B	B					B
QUIVIRA VINEYARDS '88, Dry Creek Vly. $9.25				G			S		B
RODNEY STRONG VINEYARDS '87, Charlotte's Home Vnyd. $9.00				B	S	B			
VENTANA VINEYARDS '88, Monterey $8.00				B		B	S		
VENTANA VINEYARDS '89, Monterey $8.00	G	G				B			
2 AWARDS									
ADLER FELS WINERY '89, Sonoma Co., LH $9.75	S					B			
AUDUBON CELLARS '86, Napa Vly., LH					S		B		
BANDIERA WINERY '87, Napa Co., Fume $4.25				S	B				
BENZIGER OF GLEN ELLEN '89, Sonoma Co., Fume $7.99	B					B			
BERINGER VINEYARDS '88, Knights Vly. $8.50			S						S
BERINGER VINEYARDS '88, Napa Vly., Fume $8.00			B			B			
BRUTOCAO '88, Mendocino $5.00		G				S			
BUENA VISTA WINERY '88, Lake Co.					S		G		
DAVIS BYNUM WINERY '88, Sonoma Co., Fume $7.50						B			B
CHALK HILL WINERY '87, Chalk Hill $8.00				S	S				
CHATEAU DIANA '87, Central Coast Fume	S								G
DE LOACH VINEYARDS '89, Russian River Vly. $9.00	S			G					

Sauvignon Blanc

2 AWARDS

San Diego	W. Coast	Nat'l O.S.	State Fair	Dallas	San Fran	Farmers	Orange	L.A.	
			S		S				**FALLENLEAF VINEYARDS** '88, Sonoma Vly. $8.50
		B				S			**FETZER VINEYARDS** '88, California, Valley Oaks Fume $6.49
					B	S			**GAINEY VINEYARD** '88, Santa Barbara Co. $8.75
	S		S						**E. & J. GALLO WINERY** '88, California $4.50
		S					B		**GAN EDEN WINERY** '88, Sonoma Co., Fume
	B		B						**GEYSER PEAK WINERY** '88, Sonoma Co. $5.95
S						B			**GUENOC WINERY** '87, Lake Co./Napa Co. $7.50
B	B								**GUENOC WINERY** '88, Lake Co./Napa Co.
	B	S							**BARON HERZOG WINE CELLARS** '89, Sonoma Co., Calif. Selection
					S	B			**HIDDEN CELLARS** '88, Mendocino Co. $8.50
B		B							**HUSCH VINEYARDS** '88, Mendocino., La Ribera Vnyd.
			B					S	**HUSCH VINEYARDS** '89, Mendocino, La Ribera Vnyd. $8.00
			B					B	**THOMAS JAEGER WINERY** '89, San Diego Co. $7.49
					S		B		**KENWOOD WINERY** '89, Sonoma $9.50
			S	B					**LAMBERT BRIDGE** '88, Dry Creek Vly., Fume $10.00
					G		B		**ROBERT MONDAVI WINERY** '88, Napa Vly., Fume, Reserve $15.00
					B		S		**MONTEVINA VINEYARDS** '88, California, Fume $5.75
	B		B						**OBESTER WINERY** '89, Mendocino Co. $8.50
B				B					**RAYMOND VINEYARD** '88, Napa Vly.

2 AWARDS

	L.A.	Orange	Farmers	San Fran	Dallas	State Fair	Nat'l O.S.	W. Coast	San Diego
RENAISSANCE VINEYARD '83, North Yuba, LH $20.00				S		S			
RUTHERFORD VINTNERS '87, Napa Vly. $8.00				B				B	
SANTA BARBARA WINERY '88, Santa Ynez Vly., Reserve $12.00		B		B					
SANTA BARBARA WINERY '88, Santa Ynez Vly. $9.00			B			B			
V. SATTUI WINERY '89, Napa Vly., Suzanne's Vnyd. $8.95			B					B	
CHARLES F. SHAW WINERY '88, Napa Vly.						B	S		
SHENANDOAH VINEYARDS '89, Amador $7.75	S			B					
ST. ANDREWS WINERY '87, Napa Vly. $7.50						S			B
STONE CREEK '87, Napa Vly., Special Sel. Fume	S	B							
TAFT STREET WINERY '88, Napa $7.00				S		B			
VILLA MT. EDEN WINERY '89, Napa Vly., LH	G			S					
WENTE BROS. '88, Livermore Vly., Estate Reserve $6.50				B	B				
WHITE OAK VINEYARDS '89, Sonoma Co.								S	B
WINDSOR VINEYARDS '88, Alexander Vly., SLH $15.00	S			B					

S. Anderson
NAPA VALLEY
Blanc de Noirs
NAPA VALLEY CHAMPAGNE · PRODUCED AND BOTTLED BY S. ANDERSON VINEYARD
YOUNTVILLE, CALIFORNIA U.S.A. ALC. 12.5% BY VOL. 750 ML CONTAINS SULFITES

GLORIA FERRER
1985
BRUT

Sparkling Wine

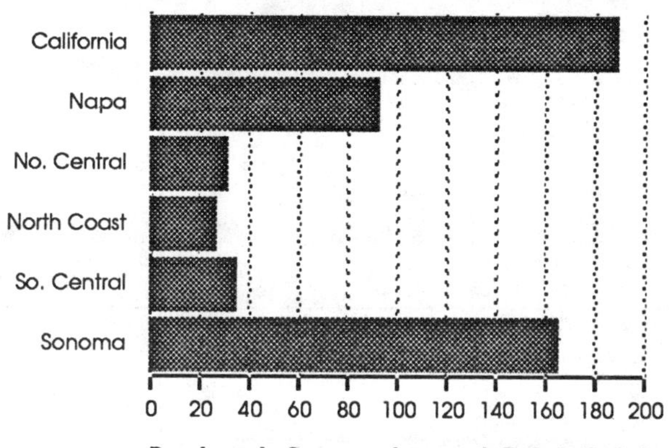

Regional Comparison of Total Points

(Gold=5   Silver=3   Bronze=1)

Highest individual wine totals

2 5 **S. ANDERSON VINEYARD**
'86, Napa, Blanc De Noirs $18.00

2 3 **GLORIA FERRER**
'85, Sonoma, Royal Cuvee $16.00

1 8 **DOMAINE MUMM**
'NV, Blanc De Noir Cuvee $15.00

1 7 **BALLATORE CHAMPAGNE CELLARS**
'NV, Calif., Gran Spumante $5.50

1 7 **CHATEAU ST. JEAN**
'87, Sonoma, Blanc De Blanc $11.00

1 7 **COOK'S CHAMPAGNE CELLARS**
'NV, American, Blush $3.99

1 7 **DOMAINE MUMM**
'NV, Cuvee, Brut Prestige $15.00

1 7 **GLORIA FERRER**
'NV, Sonoma Co. Brut $13.00

1 6 **MAISON DEUTZ WINERY**
'NV, S. Barbara/SLO, Cuvee $17.00

1 5 **JOHN CULBERTSON WINERY**
'NV, California, Cuvee Rouge $14.00

1 4 **GLORIA FERRER**
'85, Sonoma, Carneros Cuvee $20.00

1 4 **WINDSOR VINEYARDS**
'87, Sonoma Co., Brut Rose $12.00

Sparkling Wine
0 - 1.5 Residual Sugar

	L.A.	Orange	Farmers	San Fran	Dallas	State Fair	Nat'l O.S.	W. Coast	San Diego
7 AWARDS									
S. ANDERSON VINEYARD '86, Napa Vly., Blanc De Noirs $18.00	S	G		S	B	G	G		S
GLORIA FERRER '85, Sonoma Co. Royal Cuvee $16.00	S	G	G	B	S		S		S
6 AWARDS									
DOMAINE MUMM 'NV, Blanc De Noir Cuvee $15.00	S	G		B		G		S	B
GLORIA FERRER '85, Sonoma, Carneros Cuvee $20.00	S	S	B	S	B				S
KORBEL 'NV, California, Natural $12.50	B	B				B	B	B	B
MAISON DEUTZ WINERY 'NV, S. Barbara/SLO, Brut Cuvee $17.00		S	S	B		G		S	B
5 AWARDS									
CHASE-LIMOGERE 'NV, California, Brut $6.99	S		S		B	G		B	
CHATEAU DE BAUN WINERY '87, Sonoma Co., Romance $12.00			S	B		B		B	S
CHATEAU ST. JEAN '87, Sonoma, Blanc De Blanc $11.00	G	S		S		B			G
JOHN CULBERTSON WINERY 'NV, Cuvee De Frontignan $18.00		G			B	B	G		B
JOHN CULBERTSON WINERY 'NV, California, Blanc De Noir $14.00		G	S			S	B	B	
JOHN CULBERTSON WINERY 'NV, California Brut $14.00	S		B	S		B		B	
DOMAINE MUMM 'NV, Cuvee, Brut Prestige $15.00	G	S			S	S			S
GLORIA FERRER 'NV, Sonoma Co. Brut $13.00					S	S	G	S	S
MAISON DEUTZ WINERY 'NV, Santa Barbara/SLO, Rose $21.00	S	B		B	B	S			
SEBASTIANI VINEYARDS '85, Richard Cuneo Cuvee $15.00	B	B				S		S	G
SHADOW CREEK CELLARS '83, California, Brut, Reserve $16.00	S	B		B	B	S			
TOTT'S CHAMPAGNE CELLARS 'NV, California, Brut $7.50	S	G	B		B				S

Sparkling Wine
1.5 + Residual Sugar

San Diego	W. Coast	Nat'l O.S.	State Fair	Dallas	San Fran	Farmers	Orange	L.A.	
				5 AWARDS					
G	B	B				B		G	**WINDSOR VINEYARDS** '87, Sonoma Co., Blanc De Noir $13.33
				4 AWARDS					
	S		S		B	B			**JOHN CULBERTSON WINERY** '86, California, Natural $18.50
		B	B			B		B	**GREAT WESTERN WINERY** 'NV, California Blanc De Noir $8.99
G			B		B		G		**JEPSON VINEYARDS** '85, Mendocino Co., Brut $16.00
	B					S	S	B	**KORBEL** 'NV, California, Blanc De Noir $12.50
			B	S			S	B	**SHADOW CREEK CELLARS** 'NV, California, Brut $10.99
B	B	G		S					**VAN DER KAMP CHAMPAGNE** '87, Sonoma, Midnight Cuvee
	B		B			S	S		**WINDSOR VINEYARDS** '86, Sonoma Co. $12.50
		G	S				B	G	**WINDSOR VINEYARDS** '87, Sonoma Co., Brut Rose $12.00
				3 AWARDS					
S				G				B	**S. ANDERSON VINEYARD** '85, Napa Vly., Brut
			S	B		B			**COOK'S CHAMPAGNE CELLARS** 'NV, Grand Reserve Brut $5.99
B							B	B	**JOHN CULBERTSON WINERY** '86, California, Brut
	B			B				B	**JOHN CULBERTSON WINERY** '83, California, Reserve
	G			S			S		**DOMAINE MUMM** '86, Winery Lake, Brut Cuvee $24.00
B						S	S		**GREAT WESTERN WINERY** 'NV, California, Blanc De Blanc $8.99
		G	B					S	**KORBEL** 'NV, California, Brut Rose $10.50
	B	B						B	**KORBEL** 'NV, California, Blanc De Blanc
		S		B			B		**PAUL MASSON VINEYARDS** '86, Monterey, Grand Cuvee

	L.A.	Orange Farmers	San Fran Dallas	State Fair	Nat'l O.S. W. Coast	San Diego
3 AWARDS						
PARSONS CREEK WINERY 'NV, Sonoma, Tete De Cuvee $12.00	B			B	S	
WENTE BROS. '85, Arroyo Seco, Brut				B	G S	
WINDSOR VINEYARDS '86, Sonoma, Blanc De Blanc $15.00	B			B	B	
2 AWARDS						
BARONS '88, Napa, Special Cuvee		G		B		
CALLAWAY VINEYARD '85, Temecula, Blanc De Blanc		B				B
CHATEAU ST. JEAN '81, Sonoma Co.	S				B	
JOHN CULBERTSON WINERY '86, California, Brut Rose					B G	
MARK WEST VINEYARDS '84, Blanc De Noir $16.50	B	B				
MIRASSOU VINEYARDS '84, Monterey, Fifth Gen. Cuvee					B	B
PARSONS CREEK WINERY 'NV, Sonoma Co., Brut $13.00	S	B				
SEBASTIANI VINEYARDS 'NV, Sonoma Co., Blanc De Noir				B		G
SHADOW CREEK CELLARS 'NV, California, Blanc De Noirs $10.99		S		B		
M. TRIBAUT '85, Monterey Co., Rose		G				S
M. TRIBAUT 'NV, Monterey, Blanc De Noirs		B		B		

San Diego	W. Coast	Nat'l O.S.	State Fair	Dallas	San Fran	Farmers	Orange	L.A.	
						5 AWARDS			
G				S	B		G	S	**BALLATORE CHAMPAGNE CELLARS** 'NV, California, Gran Spumante $5.50
B			G			S	G	S	**COOK'S CHAMPAGNE CELLARS** 'NV, American, Blush $3.99
	S	S				B	S	G	**JOHN CULBERTSON WINERY** 'NV, California, Cuvee Rouge $14.00
						4 AWARDS			
	B	B	B					B	**CHASE-LIMOGERE** 'NV, California, Brut Rose $6.99
B			S				G	B	**COOK'S CHAMPAGNE CELLARS** 'NV, American, Extra-Dry $3.99
						3 AWARDS			
	B		B				B		**COOK'S CHAMPAGNE CELLARS** 'NV, American, White Zinfandel $4.99
S		S	B						**KORBEL** 'NV, California, Extra Dry $10.50
						B	S	G	**TOTT'S CHAMPAGNE CELLARS** 'NV, Extra Dry $7.50
						2 AWARDS			
			B				G		**CRIBARI** 'NV, Spumante Reserva $3.50
						B	B		**EAGLE RIDGE WINERY** 'NV, California, Extra Dry $6.99
			B				G		**PAUL MASSON VINEYARDS** 'NV, California, Extra Dry
			B				S		**WEIBEL VINEYARDS** 'NV, California, Sparkling Muscat $5.99

1989
GLEN·ELLEN
VINEYARDS ESTABLISHED CIRCA 1869
Proprietor's Reserve
WHITE ZINFANDEL
California

M.G.
VALLEJO
1989
CALIFORNIA
WHITE ZINFANDEL
ALCOHOL 9.2% BY VOLUME

White Zinfandel

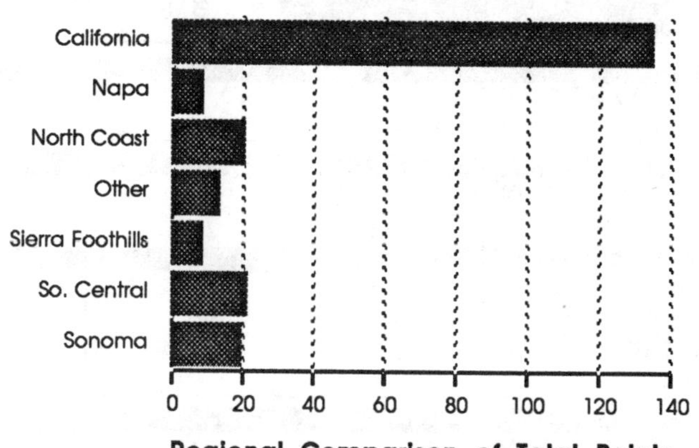

Regional Comparison of Total Points

(Gold=5   Silver=3   Bronze=1)

Highest individual wine totals

16 **BERINGER VINEYARDS**
'89, North Coast $7.00

16 **GLEN ELLEN WINERY**
'89, California, Prop. Reserve

14 **NAPA RIDGE WINERY**
'89, Lodi $5.25

13 **M. G. VALLEJO WINERY**
'89, California $4.75

11 **V. SATTUI WINERY**
'89, California $6.95

8 **CHRISTIAN BROTHERS**
'89, California

8 **FETZER VINEYARDS**
'89, California $5.99

7 **ARCIERO WINERY**
'89, Paso Robles $5.00

7 **BEL ARBORS**
'89, California, Founders Sel. $4.99

7 **MAURICE CARRIE VINEYARD**
'89, Temecula $5.50

7 **GRAND CRU VINEYARDS**
'89, California $6.50

7 **STONY RIDGE WINERY**
'89, California

White Zinfandel

	L.A.	Orange	Farmers	San Fran	Dallas	State Fair	Nat'l O.S.	W. Coast	San Diego
7 AWARDS									
M. G. VALLEJO WINERY '89, California $4.75	S	B		B		B	G	B	B
6 AWARDS									
BERINGER VINEYARDS '89, North Coast $7.00	S	B			B	S	G		S
5 AWARDS									
ARCIERO WINERY '89, Paso Robles $5.00		B		B	B		S	B	
V. SATTUI WINERY '89, California $6.95				S	B	B		S	S
4 AWARDS									
FETZER VINEYARDS '89, California $5.99		G			B	B			B
GLEN ELLEN WINERY '89, California, Proprietor's Reserve	G	G			B				G
NAPA RIDGE WINERY '89, Lodi $5.25		G	S			B	G		
3 AWARDS									
BEL ARBORS '89, California, Founders Sel. $4.99		S	S			B			
MAURICE CARRIE VINEYARD '89, Temecula $5.50		G				B		B	
CHATEAU DIANA '89, California $3.49				B			S		B
DE LOACH VINEYARDS '89, Russian River Vly. $7.00					B			S	B
GRAND CRU VINEYARDS '89, California $6.50		S		S					B
STONY RIDGE WINERY '89, California		S				B		S	
VENDANGE '89, California $4.49	B	G				B			
2 AWARDS									
BUEHLER VINEYARDS '89, Napa Vly.				S					B
CHATEAU SOUVERAIN '89, California $5.50				S		B			

White Zinfandel

2 AWARDS

San Diego	W. Coast	Nat'l O.S.	State Fair	Dallas	San Fran	Farmers	Orange	L.A.	
S							G		**CHRISTIAN BROTHERS** '89, California
							S	B	**E. & J. GALLO WINERY** '89, California
			B				B		**MADRONA VINEYARDS** '89, El Dorado $5.25
		B			G				**MONTPELLIER VINEYARDS** '89, California $5.00
			B				B		**NAVALLE SELECTIONS** '89, California $4.99
			B			B			**PARDUCCI WINE CELLARS** '89, California $5.99
		S			B				**JOSEPH PHELPS VINEYARDS** '89, California, Night Harvest $5.00
			S			S			**VALLEY OF THE MOON WINERY** '89, California $5.50
			B	B					**WILLIAM WHEELER WINERY** '89, Sonoma Co., Young Vines $6.50

TOBIN
JAMES
WINERY
1988
PASO ROBLES
ZINFANDEL
PRODUCED AND BOTTLED BY TOBIN JAMES
WINERY, PASO ROBLES, CALIFORNIA
ALC. 13.4% BY VOL. CONTAINS SULFITES
b   d

GREENWOOD
RIDGE
VINEYARDS

SONOMA COUNTY
ZINFANDEL
1988

Produced and bottled by Greenwood Ridge Vineyards,
B.W. 4960, Philo CA. Contains sulfites. Alcohol 12.5% by vol.

Zinfandel

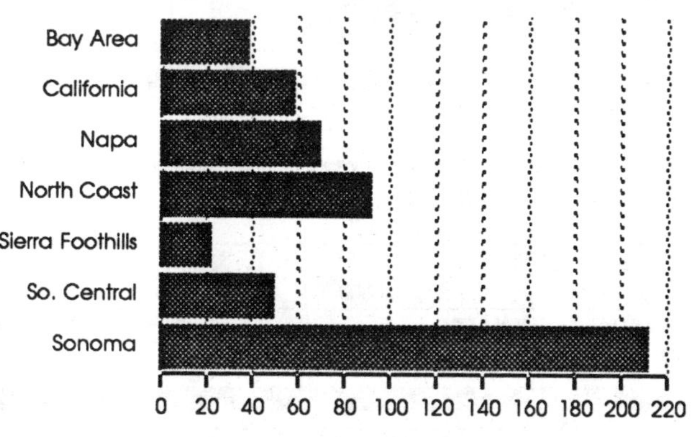

Regional Comparison of Total Points
(Gold=5   Silver=3   Bronze=1)

Highest   individual   wine   totals

1 8
CONGRESS SPRINGS VINEYARDS
'87, Santa Cruz Mtns. $12.00

1 8
TOBIN JAMES WINERY
'88, Paso Robles

1 6
GREENWOOD RIDGE VINEYARDS
'88, Sonoma Co. $10.75

1 6
GUNDLACH BUNDSCHU WINERY
'88, Rhinefarm Vnyds. $8.00

1 5
BERINGER VINEYARDS
'87, North Coast $8.00

1 4
DE LOACH VINEYARDS
'88, Russian River Vly. $10.00

1 3
OLSON WINERY
'87, Mendocino Co.

1 3
ROSENBLUM CELLARS
'88, Sonoma Co. $9.95

1 2
GLEN ELLEN WINERY
'88, Carreras Vnyd., Imagery $12.00

1 2
QUIVIRA VINEYARDS
'88, Dry Creek Vly. $12.00

1 2
ROSENBLUM CELLARS
'NV, Calif., Vintners Cuvee II $6.95

Zinfandel

	L.A.	Orange Farmers	San Fran	Dallas	State Fair	Nat'l O.S.	W. Coast	San Diego
7 AWARDS								
BERINGER VINEYARDS '87, North Coast $8.00		S	S	S	B	B	S		B
6 AWARDS								
DE LOACH VINEYARDS '88, Russian River Vly., Estate $10.00		S	B	S		S		B	S
GLEN ELLEN WINERY '88, Carreras Vnyd., Imagery $12.00		S	B		S		B	S	B
SEBASTIANI VINEYARDS '87, Sonoma Co. $6.00	B	G	B	B				B	B
5 AWARDS								
ROSENBLUM CELLARS '88, Sonoma Co. $9.95		S	B			S		G	B
4 AWARDS								
CHATEAU SOUVERAIN '87, Dry Creek Vly., Bradford Mtn. $15.00	S			B	B	B			
CONGRESS SPRINGS VINEYARDS '87, Santa Cruz Mtns., Estate $12.00					G	S	G	G	
FETZER VINEYARDS '86, Mendocino Co., Reserve $14.00	S		B	G					B
FETZER VINEYARDS '89, California $5.99		G	B	S		B			
GREENWOOD RIDGE VINEYARDS '88, Sonoma Co. $10.75						G	G	S	S
GUNDLACH BUNDSCHU WINERY '88, Sonoma Vly., Rhinefarm Vnyds. $8.00		S	G			S			G
HIDDEN CELLARS '87, Mendocino, Pacini Vnyds. $8.50	S			S		B	S		
TOBIN JAMES WINERY '88, Paso Robles		G				S	G		G
KENDALL-JACKSON WINERY '88, Mendocino, Vintner's Reserve $10.00				S	B	B			G
QUIVIRA VINEYARDS '88, Dry Creek Vly. $12.00		B	B	G				G	
RABBIT RIDGE VINEYARDS '87, Russian River Vly. $8.00				S		B	B		B
A. RAFANELLI WINERY '88, Dry Creek Vly. $9.75		B		S		B			G

Zinfandel

4 AWARDS

San Diego	W. Coast	Nat'l O.S.	State Fair	Dallas	San Fran	Farmers	Orange	L.A.	Wine
				S		B	G	S	**ROSENBLUM CELLARS** — 'NV, California, Vintners Cuvee II $6.95
					B	B	B		**STORYBOOK MT. VINEYARDS** — '87, Napa Vly. $11.50
		S		S	B				**WENTE BROS.** — '86, Raboli Vnyd., Reserve $8.00

3 AWARDS

San Diego	W. Coast	Nat'l O.S.	State Fair	Dallas	San Fran	Farmers	Orange	L.A.	Wine
	B						G		**HOP KILN WINERY** — '88, Russian River Vly. $12.00
	S				S	S			**LYTTON SPRINGS WINERY** — '88, Sonoma Co. $12.00
	B				S				**MISSION VIEW VINEYARDS** — '86, Paso Robles $8.00
G							S		**OLSON WINERY** — '87, Mendocino Co.
S				B		B			**RICHARDSON VINEYARDS** — '88, Sonoma Vly. $12.00
				B		B			**ROUND HILL CELLARS** — '87, Napa Vly. $5.50
B				B		B			**SANTINO WINES** — '86, Shenandoah Vly., Grandpere $12.00
B					B				**V. SATTUI WINERY** — '87, Napa Vly., Suzanne's Vnyd. $10.95
					S	B	B		**SEGHESIO WINERY** — '87, Northern Sonoma $6.00
				B		B			**STORYBOOK MT. VINEYARDS** — '86, Napa Vly. $12.00

2 AWARDS

San Diego	W. Coast	Nat'l O.S.	State Fair	Dallas	San Fran	Farmers	Orange	L.A.	Wine
					B				**AMADOR FOOTHILL WINERY** — '87, Grandpere Vnyd. $10.00
	S								**BOEGER WINERY** — '87, El Dorado Co., Walker Vnyd.
	S			S					**EAGLE RIDGE WINERY** — 'NV, Sonoma Coast, LH
	G								**FRANCISCAN OAKVILLE ESTATE** — '88, Napa Vly. $9.00
					S				**GUGLIELMO WINERY** — '86, Santa Clara Vly., Reserve $7.50

Zinfandel

2 AWARDS

	L.A.	Orange	Farmers	San Fran	Dallas	State Fair	Nat'l O.S.	W. Coast	San Diego
HAYWOOD WINERY '88, Sonoma Vly.		B						S	
HOP KILN WINERY '88, Sonoma Co., Primitivo $14.00		B				S			
KENDALL-JACKSON WINERY '87, Mendocino Co., Ciapusci Vnyd.		B					G		
KENWOOD WINERY '87, Sonoma, Jack London Vnyd. $12.00		S	S						
MAZZOCCO VINEYARDS '88, Sonoma Co. $13.00				B					B
MC DOWELL VALLEY VINEYARDS '88, Mc Dowell Vly. $9.50	S					S			
MIRASSOU VINEYARDS '85, California		S							G
PARDUCCI WINE CELLARS '87, North Coast $6.49					B	B			
PRESTON VINEYARDS '87, Dry Creek Vly. $10.00			B						S
RIVER RUN VINTNERS '88, California $8.00						G		S	
RIVER RUN VINTNERS '88, Cienega Vly., LH		B					B		
ROSENBLUM CELLARS 'NV, California, Vintners Cuvee III		S		S					
SANTA BARBARA WINERY '89, Santa Ynez Vly., Boujour $7.50				B		S			
SANTINO WINES '87, Shenandoah Vly., Grandpere $12.00	B			B					
V. SATTUI WINERY '84, Napa, Howell Mtn., Reserve						S	B		
V. SATTUI WINERY '86, Napa Vly, Howell Mtn. $10.95						S	G		
SAUCELITO CANYON VINEYARDS '87, San Luis Obispo Co.						G			B
TOPOLOS AT RUSSIAN RIVER '87, Sonoma Co., Rossi Ranch							B	G	
VILLA MT. EDEN WINERY '88, Napa Vly.		G		B					

Zinfandel

2 AWARDS

San Diego	W. Coast	Nat'l O.S.	State Fair	Dallas	San Fran	Farmers	Orange	L.A.	
							B		**WINDSOR VINEYARDS** '85, Russian River Vly., Winemasters Selection
		S				S			**WINDSOR VINEYARDS** '83, Russian River Vly., Reserve, LH $10.00
					B		S		**YORK MOUNTAIN WINERY** '87, San Luis Obispo $9.00

ALL VARIETALS

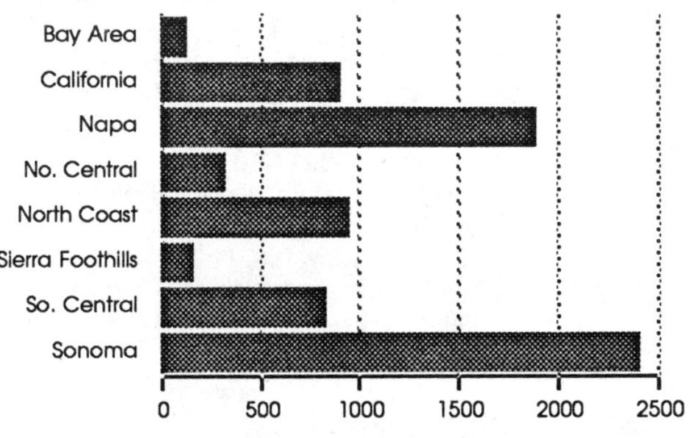

Regional Comparison of Total Points

(Gold=5   Silver=3   Bronze=1)

Highest   individual   winery   totals

2 0 1   **WINDSOR VINEYARDS**
    11455 Old Redwood Hwy., Healdsburg CA

1 8 1   **FETZER VINEYARDS**
    1150 Bel Arbes Rd., Redwood Valley CA

1 6 2   **KENDALL-JACKSON WINERY**
    700 Mathews Road, Lakeport CA 95453

1 2 4   **BENZIGER OF GLEN ELLEN**
    1883 London Ranch Rd., Glen Ellen CA

1 0 9   **CLOS DU BOIS WINES**
    5 Fitch Street, Healdsburg CA 95448

1 0 1   **DE LOACH VINEYARDS**
    1791 Olivet Rd., Santa Rosa CA 95401

9 1   **PARDUCCI WINE CELLARS**
    501 Parducci Rd., Ukiah CA 95482

9 0   **GREENWOOD RIDGE VINEYARDS**
    24555 Greenwood Road, Philo CA 95466

8 6   **RODNEY STRONG VINEYARDS**
    11455 Old Redwood Hwy., Windsor CA

8 1   **GUENOC WINERY**
    21000 Butts Canyon Rd., Middletown CA

7 7   **COSENTINO CRYSTAL VALLEY**
    7415 St. Helena Hwy., Yountville CA

7 6   **GLEN ELLEN WINERY**
    1883 London Ranch Rd., Glen Ellen CA

7 3	**FRANCISCAN OAKVILLE ESTATE** 1178 Galleron Rd., Rutherford CA 94573
7 3	**GRGICH HILLS CELLAR** 1829 St. Helena Highway, Rutherford CA
7 0	**BUENA VISTA WINERY** 27000 Ramal Road, Sonoma CA 95476
6 9	**DRY CREEK VINEYARD** 3770 Lambert Bridge Rd., Healdsburg CA
6 9	**NAVARRO VINEYARDS** 5601 Highway 128, Philo CA 95466
6 8	**CHATEAU ST. JEAN** 8555 Sonoma Hwy., Kenwood CA 95452
6 6	**GARY FARRELL WINES** P. O. Box 342, Forestville CA 95436
6 6	**HUSCH VINEYARDS** P. O. Box 189, Talmage CA 95481
6 4	**BERINGER VINEYARDS** 2000 Main Street, St Helena CA 94574
6 3	**JOHN CULBERTSON WINERY** 2608 Via Rancheros, Fallbrook CA 92028
6 2	**V. SATTUI WINERY** White Lane & Hwy. 29, St Helena CA
6 1	**CAMBRIA WINERY** Route 1, Box 142, Santa Maria CA 93454
6 1	**WHITE OAK VINEYARDS** 208 Haydon St., Healdsburg CA 95448
6 0	**SEBASTIANI VINEYARDS** 389 Fourth St. E., Sonoma CA 95476
5 9	**THOMAS FOGARTY WINERY** 5937 Alpine Road, Portola Valley CA
5 9	**KONOCTI WINERY** Hwy. 29 & Thomas, Kelseyville CA 95451
5 8	**J. LOHR WINERY** 1000 Lenzen Ave., San Jose CA 95126
5 8	**WENTE BROS.** 5565 Tesla Road, Livermore CA 94550
5 7	**GEYSER PEAK WINERY** 22281 Chianti Rd., Geyserville CA 95441
5 7	**GUNDLACH BUNDSCHU WINERY** 3775 Thornberry Road, Sonoma CA 95476
5 7	**INGLENOOK NAPA VALLEY** 100 S. St. Helena Hwy., St Helena CA
5 5	**MARKHAM VINEYARDS** 2812 N. St. Helena Hwy., St Helena CA

ACACIA WINERY
2750 Las Amigas Road Napa CA 94558
Chardonnay,'88, Napa Vly., Carneros (S-Orange)
Pinot Noir,'87, Napa Vly., Carneros, St. Clair Vnyd. (S-Orange)

ADELAIDA CELLARS
2170 Adelaida Star Road Paso Robles CA 93446
Cabernet Sauvignon,'85, Paso Robles, Central Coast (S-Dallas)
Chardonnay,'87, Paso Robles $12.75 (3)
Chardonnay,'88, Paso Robles $13.25 (3)

ADLER FELS WINERY
5325 Corrick Lane Santa Rosa CA 95405
Gewurztraminer,'89, Sonoma Co. $8.50 (B-Farmers)
Sauvignon Blanc,'88, Sonoma Co., Fume (S-Dallas)
Sauvignon Blanc,'89, Sonoma Co., Fume (B-L.A.)
Sauvignon Blanc,'89, Sonoma Co., LH $9.75 (2)

ALDERBROOK VINEYARDS
2306 Magnolia Drive Healdsburg CA 95448
Chardonnay,'88, Dry Creek Vly. (3)
Chardonnay,'88, Dry Creek Vly., Estate (S-Dallas)
Sauvignon Blanc,'88, Dry Creek Vly. (B-Dallas)

ALEXANDER VALLEY VINEYARDS
8644 Highway 128 Healdsburg CA 95448
Cabernet Sauvignon,'87, Wetzel Family Vnyd., Estate (2)

ALMADEN VINEYARDS
1530 Blossom Hill Road San Jose CA 95118
Sauvignon Blanc,'NV, California (B-Orange)

ALPEN CELLARS
Star Route 2 Trinity Center CA 96091
Johannisberg Riesling,'89, Trinity Co. (S-W.Coast)

AMADOR FOOTHILL WINERY
12500 Steiner Road Plymouth CA 95669
Sauvignon Blanc,'88, Shenandoah Vly., Fume (B-Dallas)
Sauvignon Blanc,'89, Shenandoah Vly. $9.75 (G-San Fran)
Zinfandel,'87, Shenandoah Vly., Grandpere Vnyd. $10.00 (2)

AMIZETTA VINEYARDS
1099 Greenfield Rd. St Helena CA 94574
Cabernet Sauvignon,'86, Napa Vly., Estate $17.00 (B-State Fair)

S. ANDERSON VINEYARD
1473 Yountville Creek Rd. Napa CA 94558
Chardonnay,'88, Stags Leap, Estate (2)
Sparkling Wine,'84, Napa Vly. (S-W.Coast)
Sparkling Wine,'85, Napa Vly., Brut (3)
Sparkling Wine,'86, Napa Vly., Blanc De Noirs $18.00 (7)
Sparkling Wine,'NV, Napa Vly., Rose (S-Orange)

ANTON VINEYARDS
Address not available
White Zinfandel,'89, California (B-Orange)

APTOS VINEYARD
4390 Hecker Pass Road Gilroy CA 95020
Pinot Noir,'86, Santa Cruz Co.   (S-Orange)

ARCADIA WINERY
P. O. Box 950 Lower Lake CA 95457
Cabernet Sauvignon,'84, Lake Co. $9.00 (S-State Fair)

ARCIERO WINERY
P. O. Box 1287 Paso Robles CA 93447
Cabernet Sauvignon,'86, Paso Robles, Estate   (G-Nat'l O.S.)
Chenin Blanc,'89, Paso Robles, Estate $4.50 (4)
Sauvignon Blanc,'89, Paso Robles $7.49 (3)
White Zinfandel,'89, Paso Robles $5.00 (5)

ARROWOOD
P.O. Box 987 Glen Ellen CA 95442
Cabernet Sauvignon,'86, Sonoma   (S-Orange)

VINCENT ARROYO WINERY
2361 Greenwood Ave. Calistoga CA 94515
Cabernet Sauvignon,'86, Napa Vly.   (G-Nat'l O.S.)
Cabernet Sauvignon,'87, Napa Vly., Estate   (2)
Petite Sirah,'87, Napa Vly., Estate $9.00 (3)

DAVID ARTHUR VINEYARDS
1521 Sage Canyon Road St Helena CA 94574
Chardonnay,'87, Napa Vly., Estate   (B-San Diego)

ASHLAND PARK
Address not available
Chardonnay,'89, Sonoma Co., Barrel Ferm.   (B-Orange)

AUDUBON CELLARS
600 Addison Street Berkeley CA 94710
Cabernet Sauvignon,'85, Dry Creek Vly.   (B-Dallas)
Cabernet Sauvignon,'86, Monterey Co.   (B-Orange)
Chardonnay,'87, Sonoma, Carneros, Sangiacomo $11.25 (2)
Chardonnay,'89, Napa Vly., Segas Vnyd., LH $10.99 (2)
Sauvignon Blanc,'86, Napa Vly., LH   (2)
Sauvignon Blanc,'88, Napa Vly., Pope Vnyd. $8.25 (4)
Zinfandel,'84, San Luis Obispo Co. $8.25 (B-Farmers)

AUSTIN CELLARS
1516 Copenhagen Dr. Solvang CA 93463
Johannisberg Riesling,'86, Santa Barbara, Botrytis $12.00 (B-State
Pinot Noir,'88, Santa Barbara Co.   (2)
Sauvignon Blanc,'85, Santa Barbara, Sierra Madre, Botrytis $12.00

B

BABCOCK VINEYARDS
5175 Highway 246 Lompoc CA 93436
Chardonnay,'88, Santa Ynez Vly. $16.00 (3)
Gewurztraminer,'88, Santa Barbara Co.   (S-Orange)
Johannisberg Riesling,'89, Santa Ynez, Estate, LHCS   (S-Orange)
Pinot Noir,'88, Santa Barbara Co. $12.00 (3)
Sauvignon Blanc,'88, Santa Ynez Vly., Estate   (B-Orange)

BAILY VINEYARD

36150 Pauba Road Temecula CA 92390

Johannisberg Riesling,'89, Temecula, Mother's Vnyd. $7.50 (2)
Meritage White,'89, Temecula, Montage $10.00 (4)

BALDINELLI VINEYARDS

10801 Dickson Rd. Plymouth CA 95669

Sauvignon Blanc,'89, California $7.50 (B-San Fran)

BALLARD CANYON WINERY

1825 Ballard Canyon Rd. Solvang CA 93463

Chardonnay,'89, Santa Barbara Co., Dr.'s Fun Baby (B-Orange)
Chardonnay,'89, Santa Ynez Vly., Reserve (G-L.A.)
Johannisberg Riesling,'89, Reserve (S-L.A.)
Johannisberg Riesling,'89, Santa Ynez Vly., Estate (3)

BALLATORE CHAMPAGNE CELLARS

P. O. Box 1130 Modesto CA 95353

Sparkling Wine,'NV, California, Gran Spumante $5.50 (5)

BALVERNE WINERY

10810 Hillview Road Windsor CA 95492

Cabernet Sauvignon,'84, Chalk Hill, Laurel Vnyd. $12.00 (3)
Chardonnay,'88, Chalk Hill $9.50 (2)
Sauvignon Blanc,'88, Chalk Hill, Stonecrest Vnyd. $6.50 (3)

BANDIERA WINERY

155 Cherry Creek Rd. Cloverdale CA 95425

Cabernet Sauvignon,'86, Napa Vly. $6.50 (2)
Sauvignon Blanc,'87, Napa Co., Fume $4.25 (2)

BAREFOOT CELLARS

8075-B Westside Road Healdsburg CA 95448

Cabernet Sauvignon,'NV, California $4.99 (6)

BARGETTO WINERY

3535 N. Main Street Soquel CA 95073

Cabernet Sauvignon,'87, Napa Vly., Cypress $9.75 (5)
Cabernet Sauvignon,'88, California Cabernet Table Wine $5.50 (2)
Chardonnay,'88, Santa Cruz Mtns. $18.00 (3)
Chardonnay,'89, Central Coast, Cypress (2)
Pinot Noir,'87, Sierra Madre/Bien Nacido Vnyds. $16.00 (2)
White Zinfandel,'89, Sonoma Co. $7.50 (B-Farmers)

BARONS

Address not available

Sparkling Wine,'88, Napa, Special Cuvee (2)

BEAULIEU VINEYARD

1960 St. Helena Highway Rutherford CA 94573

Cabernet Sauvignon,'85, Napa Vly., Georges De Latour, Reserve
Cabernet Sauvignon,'86, Napa Vly., Rutherford $9.50 (2)
Cabernet Sauvignon,'87, Napa Vly., Beau Tour (S-Orange)
Chardonnay,'88, Carneros, Reserve (2)
Chardonnay,'88, Napa Vly., Beaufort (B-Orange)
Pinot Noir,'88, Napa Vly., Beaumont (B-Orange)
Pinot Noir,'88, Napa Vly., Carneros Reserve $9.50 (5)
Sauvignon Blanc,'88, Napa Vly, Estate (4)
Sauvignon Blanc,'89, Napa Vly., Estate $8.50 (S-State Fair)

BEL ARBORS

13325 S. Highway 101 Hopland CA 95449

Cabernet Sauvignon,'NV, American, Founder's Sel. $5.49 (4)
Chardonnay,'NV, American (G-Nat'l O.S.)
Merlot,'NV, American $6.00 (2)
White Zinfandel,'89, California, Founders Sel. $4.99 (3)

BELL RANCH

Address not available

Cabernet Sauvignon,'86, Sonoma Vly., Estate   (S-Orange)

BELVEDERE WINERY

4035 Westside Road Healdsburg CA 95448

Chardonnay,'88, Carneros, Reserve $12.00 (2)
Chardonnay,'89, Sonoma Co., Discovery (B-Orange)
Merlot,'87, Alexander Vly. $12.00 (S-Farmers)
Sauvignon Blanc,'88, North Coast (B-W.Coast)

BENZIGER OF GLEN ELLEN

1883 London Ranch Rd. Glen Ellen CA 95442

Cabernet Sauvignon,'86, Sonoma Vly., Estate (2)
Cabernet Sauvignon,'87, Sonoma Co. $10.00 (3)
Cabernet Sauvignon,'87, Sonoma Co., Estate (2)
Chardonnay,'88, Sonoma Co. $10.00 (5)
Meritage Red,'87, Sonoma Mtn., A Tribute $25.00 (9)
Meritage White,'88, Sonoma, Estate $15.00 (4)
Merlot,'86, Sonoma Co. (2)
Merlot,'87, Sonoma Vly., Estate $15.00 (7)
Sauvignon Blanc,'88, Sonoma Co. (4)
Sauvignon Blanc,'89, Sonoma Co., Fume $7.99 (2)

BERGFIELD CELLARS

401 So. St. Helena Hwy. St Helena CA 94574

Merlot,'87, Napa Vly. $12.00 (3)

BERINGER VINEYARDS

2000 Main Street St Helena CA 94574

Cabernet Sauvignon,'84, Napa Vly., Chabot Vnyd. (B-Dallas)
Cabernet Sauvignon,'85, Napa Vly., Chabot Vnyd. (G-Nat'l O.S.)
Cabernet Sauvignon,'85, Napa Vly., Reserve (B-Dallas)
Chardonnay,'88, Napa Vly., Estate (S-Nat'l O.S.)
Chardonnay,'88, Napa Vly., Estate Reserve $18.50 (2)
Chenin Blanc,'88, Napa Vly. $6.50 (B-Farmers)
Gewurztraminer,'89, North Coast $5.25 (3)
Johannisberg Riesling,'89, North Coast (S-Nat'l O.S.)
Sauvignon Blanc,'88, Knights Vly. $8.50 (2)
Sauvignon Blanc,'88, Napa Vly., Fume $8.00 (2)
Sauvignon Blanc,'89, Napa Vly. (G-L.A.)
White Zinfandel,'89, North Coast $7.00 (6)
Zinfandel,'87, North Coast $8.00 (7)

BLACK MOUNTAIN VINEYARD

P.O. Box 921 Healdsburg CA 95448

Cabernet Sauvignon,'85, Alexander Vly. $18.00 (4)
Chardonnay,'87, Alexander Vly., Gravel Bar (B-San Diego)
Chardonnay,'88, Alexander Vly., Douglas Hill $10.00 (2)

BLOSSOM HILL COLLECTION
P. O. Box 391 St Helena CA 94574
Sauvignon Blanc,'89, California (G-Orange)

BOEGER WINERY
1709 Carson Road Placerville CA 95667
Merlot,'87, El Dorado, Estate $12.50 (2)
Zinfandel,'87, El Dorado Co., Walker Vnyd. (2)

BOGLE VINEYARDS
Rt. 1, Box 276 Clarksburg CA 95612
Chardonnay,'89, California (S-Orange)
Merlot,'89, California $7.50 (2)
White Zinfandel,'89, California (B-Orange)
Zinfandel,'89, California (S-Orange)

BOUCHAINE VINEYARDS
1975 Buchli Sta. Rd. Napa CA 94558
Chardonnay,'86, Napa Vly., Carneros, Estate Reserve (S-Dallas)
Chardonnay,'87, Carneros $16.00 (2)
Chardonnay,'88, Carneros $16.00 (B-San Fran)
Pinot Noir,'87, Napa Vly., Carneros $15.00 (4)
Pinot Noir,'87, Napa Vly., Carneros, Reserve $19.00 (2)

BOYER
Address not available
Chardonnay,'88, Monterey Co., Ventana Vnyd. $13.50 (2)

BRAREN PAULI WINERY
1613 Spring Hill Road Petaluma CA 94952
Cabernet Sauvignon,'87, Dry Creek Vly., Mauritson Vnyd. $11.50 (6)
Cabernet Sauvignon,'87, Mendocino (2)
Merlot,'87, Alexander Vly., Mauritson Vnyd. $12.50 (5)

BRICELAND VINEYARDS
5959 Briceland Rd. Redway CA 95560
Johannisberg Riesling,'89, Anderson Vly., Dennison Vnyd. $9.00 (2)
Sauvignon Blanc,'89, Anderson Vly, Ferrington Vnyd. (B-Orange)

DAVID BRUCE WINERY
21439 Bear Creek Red. Los Gatos CA 95030
Cabernet Sauvignon,'85, Vintner's Select (B-Dallas)

BRUTOCAO
Hwy. 175 Hopland CA 95445
Cabernet Sauvignon,'82, (G-L.A.)
Cabernet Sauvignon,'84, (S-L.A.)
Cabernet Sauvignon,'86, Mendocino $9.00 (2)
Chardonnay,'88, Mendocino $9.00 (2)
Sauvignon Blanc,'88, Mendocino $5.00 (2)

BUEHLER VINEYARDS
820 Greenfield Rd. St Helena CA 94574
Cabernet Sauvignon,'87, Napa Vly., Estate (S-W.Coast)
White Zinfandel,'89, Napa Vly. (2)

BUENA VISTA WINERY
27000 Ramal Road Sonoma CA 95476
Cabernet Sauvignon,'86, Carneros, Reserve $22.50 (2)
Cabernet Sauvignon,'87, Carneros, Estate (G-W.Coast)
Chardonnay,'87, Carneros, Reserve (2)

Chardonnay,'88, Carneros, Reserve (B-Orange)
Chardonnay,'89, Carneros (B-L.A.)
Gewurztraminer,'87, Carneros, Estate (5)
Johannisberg Riesling,'88, Carneros (2)
Merlot,'86, Carneros, Estate Reserve (B-Dallas)
Merlot,'87, Carneros, Estate Reserve $16.50 (2)
Pinot Noir,'87, Carneros, Estate Reserve (2)
Sauvignon Blanc,'87, Alexander Vly., Fume (G-Dallas)
Sauvignon Blanc,'88, Lake Co. (2)
Sauvignon Blanc,'88, Mendocino Co. (S-Dallas)
Sauvignon Blanc,'89, Lake Co. $8.50 (5)

BURGESS CELLARS

1108 Deer Park Rd. St Helena CA 94574
Cabernet Sauvignon,'86, Napa Vly., Vintage Selection (2)
Chardonnay,'88, Napa Vly., Triere Vnyd. (S-Orange)
Zinfandel,'87, Napa Vly. (B-San Diego)

DAVIS BYNUM WINERY

8075 Westside Road Healdsburg CA 95448
Cabernet Sauvignon,'87, Sonoma Co. (B-Dallas)
Chardonnay,'88, Russian River Vly. $16.00 (2)
Gewurztraminer,'89, Russian River Vly., McIlroy Vnyd. $8.00 (5)
Pinot Noir,'87, Russian River Vly. $16.00 (5)
Sauvignon Blanc,'88, Sonoma Co., Fume $7.50 (2)

BYRON VINEYARD

5230 Tepusquet Rd. Santa Maria CA 93454
Chardonnay,'87, Barrel Ferm., Reserve $16.00 (B-Farmers)
Chardonnay,'88, Santa Barbara Co. (4)
Pinot Noir,'87, Santa Barbara Co. (B-W.Coast)
Pinot Noir,'87, Santa Barbara Co., Reserve $16.00 (3)
Pinot Noir,'88, Santa Barbara Co. (S-L.A.)
Sauvignon Blanc,'89, Santa Barbara (3)

C

CACHE CELLARS

Rt. 2 Box 2780 Davis CA 95616
Cabernet Sauvignon,'86, Napa Vly. $12.00 (S-State Fair)

CAFARO

Address not available
Cabernet Sauvignon,'87, Napa Vly. (B-Orange)
Merlot,'88, Napa Vly. (S-Orange)

CAIN CELLARS

3800 Langtry Rd. St Helena CA 94574
Cabernet Sauvignon,'86, Napa Vly. (S-Orange)
Chardonnay,'87, Napa Vly. (B-Dallas)
Chardonnay,'88, Napa Vly., Carneros $16.00 (2)
Meritage Red,'86, Napa, Cain Five $30.00 (3)

CAKEBREAD CELLARS

8300 St. Helena Hwy. Rutherford CA 94573
Cabernet Sauvignon,'87, Napa Vly. (B-Orange)
Sauvignon Blanc,'89, Napa Vly. (S-Orange)

CALERA
11300 Cienega Rd. Hollister CA 95023
Pinot Noir,'87, San Benito Co., Jensen (B-Orange)
Pinot Noir,'87, San Benito Co., Mills, Young Vines (B-Orange)

CALLAWAY VINEYARD
32720 Rancho California Rd. Temecula CA 92390
Chenin Blanc,'88, Temecula, Morning Harvest (2)
Chenin Blanc,'89, Temecula, Morning Harvest, Dry $6.50 (3)
Johannisberg Riesling,'89, Temecula (B-W.Coast)
Sauvignon Blanc,'87, Temecula, Fume $8.00 (B-Farmers)
Sparkling Wine,'85, Temecula, Blanc De Blanc (2)

CAMBRIA WINERY
Route 1, Box 142 Santa Maria CA 93454
Chardonnay,'86, Santa Barbara Co., Reserve (G-Dallas)
Chardonnay,'88, Santa Barbara Co., Cambria $15.00 (3)
Chardonnay,'88, Santa Maria Vly., Reserve $25.00 (5)
Chardonnay,'89, Santa Maria Vly., Katherine's Vnyd. $16.00 (4)
Pinot Noir,'88, Santa Maria Vly., Julia's Vnyd. $16.00 (6)

J. CAREY CELLARS
1711 Alamo Pintado Road Solvang CA 93463
Cabernet Sauvignon,'86, Santa Ynez, La Cuesta Vnyd. $13.00 (4)
Chardonnay,'88, Santa Ynez Vly. $12.00 (3)
Merlot,'86, Santa Ynez Vly., La Cuesta Vnyd. (B-San Diego)
Pinot Noir,'87, Santa Ynez Vly. $10.00 (2)
Sauvignon Blanc,'88, Santa Ynez Vly. $9.00 (3)

CARMENET
1700 Moon Mountain Road Sonoma CA 95476
Meritage Red,'87, Sonoma Vly., Estate (G-Orange)
Meritage White,'87, Edna Vly. (G-Orange)

CARNEROS CREEK WINERY
1285 Dealy Lane Napa CA 94559
Chardonnay,'88, Los Carneros (2)
Pinot Noir,'88, Los Carneros, Fleur De Carneros (B-Dallas)

CARNEROS QUALITY ALLIANCE
Address not available
Pinot Noir,'86, Los Carneros (B-Dallas)

MAURICE CARRIE VINEYARD
34225 Rancho Calif. Rd. Temecula CA 92390
Chardonnay,'88, Temecula (B-Dallas)
Johannisberg Riesling,'89, Temecula (B-W.Coast)
Merlot,'86, Santa Barbara (G-Orange)
White Zinfandel,'89, Temecula $5.50 (3)

CASA NUESTRA
3473 Silverado Trail N. St Helena CA 94574
Chenin Blanc,'87, LH (B-L.A.)
Johannisberg Riesling,'89, Napa Vly., Estate (B-Orange)

CASTORO CELLARS
P. O. Box 1973 Atascadero CA 93423
Cabernet Sauvignon,'87, Paso Robles, Hope Farms (2)
Pinot Noir,'88, Santa Barbara $9.50 (4)
Zinfandel,'87, Paso Robles (G-Dallas)

Zinfandel,'88, Paso Robles $8.00 (B-San Fran)

CASWELL VINEYARDS

13207 Dupont Road Sebastopol CA 95472

Gewurztraminer,'87, Russian River Vly. (G-Dallas)

CAYMUS VINEYARDS

8700 Conn Creek Road Rutherford CA 94573

Cabernet Sauvignon,'86, Napa Vly, Cuvee (S-Orange)
Sauvignon Blanc,'88, Napa $9.00 (B-San Fran)
Zinfandel,'87, Napa Vly. (B-Dallas)

CHALK HILL WINERY

10300 Chalk Hill Rd. Healdsburg CA 95448

Chardonnay,'88, (S-Nat'l O.S.)
Sauvignon Blanc,'85, Chalk Hill, LH $10.00 (4)
Sauvignon Blanc,'87, Chalk Hill $8.00 (2)
Sauvignon Blanc,'88, Chalk Hill $8.00 (S-San Fran)

CHAMISAL VINEYARD

7525 Orcutt Rd. San Luis Obispo CA 93401

Chardonnay,'88, Edna Vly., Estate (B-San Diego)

CHANDON

California Dr. Yountville CA 94599

Sparkling Wine,'NV, Blanc De Noirs (S-Orange)
Sparkling Wine,'NV, Brut (S-Orange)

CHAPPELLET VINEYARD

1581 Sage Canyon Road St Helena CA 94574

Cabernet Sauvignon,'84, Napa Vly., Signature (B-Dallas)
Chardonnay,'87, Napa Vly. $14.00 (5)
Chenin Blanc,'86, Napa Vly., Dry (B-Dallas)
Chenin Blanc,'87, Napa Vly., Dry (B-Orange)

CHASE-LIMOGERE

P.O. Box 55 Woodbridge CA 95258

Sparkling Wine,'NV, California, Brut $6.99 (5)
Sparkling Wine,'NV, California, Brut Rose $6.99 (4)

CHATEAU DE BAUN WINERY

P.O. Box 11483 Santa Rosa CA 95406

Sparkling Wine,'87, Sonoma Co., Rhapsody (B-W.Coast)
Sparkling Wine,'87, Sonoma Co., Romance $12.00 (5)

CHATEAU DE LEU WINERY

1635 W. Mason Road Suisun CA 94585

Chardonnay,'88, Green Vly., Solano, Estate $8.95 (2)

CHATEAU DIANA

443 Allan Court Healdsburg CA 95448

Johannisberg Riesling,'89, Monterey $3.99 (B-State Fair)
Sauvignon Blanc,'87, Central Coast Fume (2)
White Zinfandel,'89, California $3.49 (3)

CHATEAU JULIEN

8940 Carmel Valley Rd. Carmel CA 93923

Cabernet Sauvignon,'82, Monterey Co., Reserve $17.00 (2)
Cabernet Sauvignon,'86, Monterey Co., Reserve $17.00 (3)
Cabernet Sauvignon,'88, Central Coast $5.00 (B-San Fran)
Chardonnay,'89, Monterey Co., Barrel Ferm. (B-San Diego)

CHATEAU NAPA BEAUCANON
1695 St. Helena Hwy. St Helena CA 94574
Chardonnay,'87, Napa Vly. (B-Dallas)
Chardonnay,'88, Napa Vly. (B-Orange)

CHATEAU POTELLE
845 Oak Grove Ave., #115 Menlo Park CA 94025
Chardonnay,'88, Carneros (B-San Diego)
Sauvignon Blanc,'88, Napa $8.25 (B-San Fran)

CHATEAU SOUVERAIN
400 Souverain Road Geyserville CA 95441
Cabernet Sauvignon,'86, Alexander Vly. (2)
Cabernet Sauvignon,'87, Alexander Vly. $9.50 (B-Farmers)
Chardonnay,'87, Sonoma, Carneros, Reserve (2)
Chardonnay,'88, Sonoma Co. (B-Orange)
Chardonnay,'88, Sonoma, Carneros, Reserve $13.00 (2)
Merlot,'87, Sonoma Co. (2)
White Zinfandel,'89, California $5.50 (2)
Zinfandel,'87, Dry Creek Vly., Bradford Mtn. $15.00 (4)

CHATEAU ST. JEAN
8555 Sonoma Hwy. Kenwood CA 95452
Cabernet Sauvignon,'86, Alexander Vly. $19.00 (3)
Gewurztraminer,'86, Alexander Vly., Belle Terre, SLH $14.00 (3)
Gewurztraminer,'89, Sonoma Co. $8.00 (2)
Johannisberg Riesling,'88, Alexander Vly., SLH $20.00 (6)
Johannisberg Riesling,'89, Sonoma Co. $9.00 (2)
Sauvignon Blanc,'88, Russian River, La Petite Etoile $10.50 (3)
Sparkling Wine,'81, Sonoma Co. (2)
Sparkling Wine,'87, Sonoma, Blanc De Blanc $11.00 (5)

CHATEAU THOMAS WINERY
Address not available
Merlot,'85, Napa Vly. (B-San Diego)

CHATOM VINEYARDS
7449 Esmeralda Road San Andreas CA 95249
Cabernet Sauvignon,'87, Calaveras Co. $10.00 (B-State Fair)
Chardonnay,'88, Calaveras Co. (B-L.A.)
Sauvignon Blanc,'87, Calaveras Co., Fume (B-Orange)

CHESTNUT HILL
75 Broadway, Suite 207 San Francisco CA 94111
Cabernet Sauvignon,'87, Sonoma Co. (B-Orange)
Merlot,'87, Napa Vly. (S-San Diego)

CHOUINARD VINEYARDS
33853 Palomares Road Castro Valley CA 94552
Cabernet Sauvignon,'87, Arroyo Seco (B-San Diego)

CHRISTIAN BROTHERS
P. O. Box 391 St Helena CA 94574
Cabernet Sauvignon,'86, Napa Vly. $10.00 (3)
Chardonnay,'87, Napa Vly., Estate Reserve $12.00 (B-State Fair)
Chardonnay,'88, Napa $8.50 (3)
Merlot,'86, Napa Vly. $8.50 (4)
White Zinfandel,'89, California (2)
Zinfandel,'87, Napa Vly. (B-Orange)

CILURZO VINEYARD
41220 Calle Contento Temecula CA 92390
Chenin Blanc,'89, Temecula $6.00 (2)
Petite Sirah,'84, Unfiltered, Estate   (S-Nat'l O.S.)

CLINE CELLARS
Rt. 2, Box 175C, Seller Ave. Oakley CA 94561
Zinfandel,'87, LH $14.00 (S-Farmers)

CLOS DU BOIS WINES
5 Fitch Street Healdsburg CA 95448
Cabernet Sauvignon,'81, Alexander Vly., Briarcrest   (G-Nat'l O.S.)
Cabernet Sauvignon,'86, Alexander Vly., Briarcrest   (2)
Cabernet Sauvignon,'87, Alexander Vly. $12.00 (4)
Chardonnay,'87, Alexander Vly., Reserve $24.00 (6)
Chardonnay,'88, Alexander Vly. $12.00 (2)
Chardonnay,'88, Alexander Vly., Calcaire $16.00 (3)
Chardonnay,'88, Dry Creek Vly., Flintwood $18.00 (4)
Gewurztraminer,'89, Alexander Vly., Early Harvest $8.00 (2)
Gewurztraminer,'89, Alexander Vly., LH $18.00 (S-L.A.)
Gewurztraminer,'89, Fleur D'Alexandra, LH $18.00 (2)
Meritage Red,'86, Alexander Vly., Marlstone $19.00 (7)
Merlot,'87, Sonoma Co. $12.00 (7)
Pinot Noir,'87, Sonoma Co. $11.99 (3)
Pinot Noir,'88, Sonoma Co.   (S-L.A.)

CLOS DU MURIEL
40620 Calle Contento Temecula CA 92390
Chardonnay,'88, California, Reserve (B-Orange)
Johannisberg Riesling,'89, Temecula $6.99 (3)
Sauvignon Blanc,'89, Estate   (S-L.A.)
White Zinfandel,'89,   (S-Nat'l O.S.)

CLOS DU VAL WINE CO.
5330 Silverado Trail Napa CA 94558
Cabernet Sauvignon,'86, Napa Vly., Estate $16.00 (6)
Cabernet Sauvignon,'86, Napa Vly., Joli Val (B-Nat'l O.S.)
Cabernet Sauvignon,'87, Napa Vly., Joli Val (S-Orange)
Chardonnay,'88, Napa Vly., Carneros, Estate $14.00 (2)
Chardonnay,'88, Napa Vly., Joli Val (B-Dallas)
Merlot,'87, Napa Vly., Stags Leap, Estate $17.00 (3)
Pinot Noir,'87, Napa Vly. (B-Dallas)
Zinfandel,'87, Napa Vly., Stags Leap, Estate $12.00 (B-San Fran)

CLOS PEGASE WINERY
1060 Dunaweal Lane Calistoga CA 94515
Cabernet Sauvignon,'86, Napa Vly. $17.00 (3)
Chardonnay,'87, Los Carneros $15.50 (5)
Chardonnay,'87, Napa Vly. $13.00 (5)
Chardonnay,'88, Napa Vly. $12.00 (B-State Fair)
Sauvignon Blanc,'87, Lake Co. (G-San Diego)
Sauvignon Blanc,'87, Napa Vly., Fume $9.50 (3)

B. R. COHN
P.O. Box 1673 Sonoma CA 95476
Cabernet Sauvignon,'87, Sonoma Vly., Olive Hill Vnyd.   (S-Orange)

CONCANNON VINEYARD
4590 Tesla Road Livermore CA 94550
Chardonnay,'87, California $11.25 (B-San Fran)
Meritage White,'87, Livermore Vly., Assemblage (2)
Petite Sirah,'86, Livermore Vly., Estate (B-Orange)

CONGRESS SPRINGS VINEYARDS
23600 Congress Springs Rd. Saratoga CA 95070
Chardonnay,'88, Santa Clara Co. $12.50 (2)
Chardonnay,'88, Santa Clara Vly., San Ysidro, Reserve (2)
Pinot Noir,'88, Santa Clara Co. $10.00 (2)
Zinfandel,'87, Santa Cruz Mtns., Estate $12.00 (4)

CONN CREEK WINERY
8711 Silverado Trail St Helena CA 94574
Cabernet Sauvignon,'85, Napa Vly. $13.00 (4)
Cabernet Sauvignon,'85, Napa Vly., Reserve (S-Nat'l O.S.)
Cabernet Sauvignon,'86, Napa Vly., Reserve $15.00 (B-State Fair)
Merlot,'87, Napa Vly., Barrel Select, Collins Vnyd. (3)
Sauvignon Blanc,'87, Napa Vly. $10.00 (S-San Fran)

R. & J. COOK
Netherlands Road Clarksburg CA 95612
Chenin Blanc,'89, Clarksburg, Estate, Dry $5.50 (B-Farmers)
Merlot,'87, Clarksburg, Estate (B-Orange)

COOK'S CHAMPAGNE CELLARS
1 Winemasters Way Lodi CA 95241
Sparkling Wine,'NV, American, Blush $3.99 (5)
Sparkling Wine,'NV, American, Extra-Dry $3.99 (4)
Sparkling Wine,'NV, American, White Zinfandel $4.99 (3)
Sparkling Wine,'NV, Grand Reserve Brut $5.99 (3)

CORBETT CANYON VINEYARDS
Corbett Canyon Rd. San Luis Obispo CA 93406
Cabernet Sauvignon,'87, Central Coast, Reserve $8.50 (2)
Cabernet Sauvignon,'87, Central Coat, Classic (G-Orange)
Chardonnay,'88, Central Coast, Classic $15.00 (2)
Chardonnay,'88, Central Coast, Reserve $8.25 (3)
Pinot Noir,'88, Central Coast, Estate $15.00 (2)
Pinot Noir,'88, Central Coast, Reserve $8.25 (3)
Sauvignon Blanc,'89, Central Coast, Reserve $5.25 (B-State Fair)
Sauvignon Blanc,'89, Central Coast/California (G-W.Coast)
White Zinfandel,'89, Central Coast, Classic (B-Orange)

COSENTINO CRYSTAL VALLEY
7415 St. Helena Hwy. Yountville CA 94599
Cabernet Sauvignon,'86, North Coast (B-Dallas)
Cabernet Sauvignon,'86, North Coast, Reserve (3)
Cabernet Sauvignon,'87, North Coast $16.00 (4)
Cabernet Sauvignon,'87, North Coast/Sonoma Co. $14.00 (6)
Chardonnay,'88, Napa Co. (S-Nat'l O.S.)
Chardonnay,'89, North Coast/Napa Co. $14.00 (2)
Meritage Red,'87, California, The Poet $25.00 (6)
Merlot,'87, Napa Co. (B-Orange)
Merlot,'88, California $17.00 (6)
Petite Sirah,'87, Napa Vly., The Butcher (B-Dallas)

CRESCINI WINES
2621 Old San Jose Rd. Soquel CA 95073
Petite Sirah,'86, Santa Clara Co. (B-Dallas)
CRESTON MANOR VINEYARD
17 Mile Post, Hwy. 58 Creston CA 93432
Cabernet Sauvignon,'86, Paso Robles, Winemaker's $19.50 (3)
Cabernet Sauvignon,'86, San Luis Obispo Co. $10.00 (2)
Chardonnay,'88, Paso Robles (2)
Meritage White,'88, Paso Robles (S-W.Coast)
Pinot Noir,'89, Paso Robles, Petit D'Noir $9.00 (2)
CRIBARI
3223 E. Church Ave. Fresno CA 93714
Sparkling Wine,'NV, Spumante Reserva $3.50 (2)
White Zinfandel,'NV, California (B-Orange)
CRICHTON HALL ESTATE
P. O. Box 187 Rutherford CA 94573
Chardonnay,'87, Napa Vly. (S-Dallas)
Chardonnay,'88, Napa Vly. (3)
JOHN CULBERTSON WINERY
2608 Via Rancheros Fallbrook CA 92028
Sparkling Wine,'83, California, Reserve (3)
Sparkling Wine,'86, California, Brut (3)
Sparkling Wine,'86, California, Brut Rose (2)
Sparkling Wine,'86, California, Natural $18.50 (4)
Sparkling Wine,'NV, California Brut $14.00 (5)
Sparkling Wine,'NV, California, Blanc De Noir $14.00 (5)
Sparkling Wine,'NV, California, Cuvee Rouge $14.00 (5)
Sparkling Wine,'NV, Cuvee De Frontignan $18.00 (5)
CUVAISON
4550 Silverado Trail Calistoga CA 94515
Cabernet Sauvignon,'87, Napa Vly. (B-Orange)

D

DA VINCI VINEYARD
Address not available
Cabernet Sauvignon,'82, Sierra Foothills, Estate $9.50 (B-State Fair)
DALLE VALLE VINEYARDS
7776 Silverado Trail Yountville CA 94599
Cabernet Sauvignon,'86, Napa Vly. (B-Orange)
DE LOACH VINEYARDS
1791 Olivet Rd. Santa Rosa CA 95401
Chardonnay,'88, Russian River Vly. $15.00 (5)
Gewurztraminer,'88, Russian River Vly., Early Harvest $7.50 (2)
Gewurztraminer,'89, Russian River Vly. $7.50 (3)
Gewurztraminer,'89, Russian River Vly., LH $12.00 (6)
Pinot Noir,'86, Russian River, Estate (S-Nat'l O.S.)
Pinot Noir,'87, Russian River Vly., Estate (B-San Diego)
Sauvignon Blanc,'88, Russian River Vly. (G-Nat'l O.S.)
Sauvignon Blanc,'89, Russian River Vly. $9.00 (2)
Sauvignon Blanc,'89, Russian River Vly., Fume $9.00 (3)
White Zinfandel,'89, Russian River Vly. $7.00 (3)
Zinfandel,'88, Russian River Vly., Estate $10.00 (6)

DE LORIMER WINERY

P.O. Box 726 Geyserville CA 95441

Chardonnay,'87, Alexander Vly. (S-Dallas)
Chardonnay,'88, Alexander Vly., Prism $13.50 (2)
Meritage Red,'87, Paso Robles, Mosaic $15.00 (B-State Fair)
Meritage White,'88, Alexander Vly., Estate, Spectrum $8.50 (3)

DE MOOR WINERY

P. O. Box 348 Oakville CA 94562

Chenin Blanc,'89, Napa Vly. $6.25 (4)
Sauvignon Blanc,'87, Napa Vly., Fie Doux $11.00 (B-Farmers)

DEER PARK WINERY

1000 Deer Park Rd. Deer Park CA 94576

Zinfandel,'86, Napa Vly., Le Blanc Vnyd. (B-San Diego)

DEER VALLEY VINEYARDS

P.O. Box 780 Gonzales CA 93926

Cabernet Sauvignon,'86, California (2)
White Zinfandel,'89, California (B-W.Coast)

DEHLINGER WINERY

6300 Guerneville Road Sebastopol CA 95472

Cabernet Sauvignon,'86, Russian River Vly., Estate $13.00 (2)
Chardonnay,'88, Russian River Vly., Estate $12.00 (5)
Pinot Noir,'87, Russian River Vly., Estate $14.00 (7)

DELICATO VINEYARDS

12001 S. Hwy. 99 Manteca CA 95336

Cabernet Sauvignon,'87, California (B-San Diego)
Chardonnay,'88, California $6.50 (2)
Sauvignon Blanc,'88, California (B-Orange)
Sauvignon Blanc,'NV, California, Proprietor's $8.50 (B-Farmers)

DEUX AMIS

Address not available

Zinfandel,'88, Sonoma Co. (B-Orange)

DEVLIN WINE CELLARS

P. O. Box 728 Soquel CA 95073

Cabernet Sauvignon,'86, Monterey, Smith & Hook (B-Orange)
Johannisberg Riesling,'89, Monterey, Arroyo Seco (B-Orange)
Merlot,'86, Central Coast $9.00 (B-State Fair)
Sauvignon Blanc,'88, Central Coast (S-Orange)
Zinfandel,'86, Santa Cruz Mtns., Beaurgard Ranch (B-San Diego)

DION VINEYARDS

P. O. Box 728 Soquel CA 95073

Chardonnay,'87, Sonoma $10.50 (S-San Fran)

DOMAINE BRETON

Address not available

Chardonnay,'89, California (S-Orange)

DOMAINE MICHEL

4155 Wine Creek Road Healdsburg CA 95448

Cabernet Sauvignon,'86, Sonoma Co. $19.50 (6)
Chardonnay,'86, Sonoma Co. $16.00 (S-Farmers)

DOMAINE MUMM
1111 Dunaweal Ln. Calistoga CA 94515
Sparkling Wine,'86, Winery Lake, Brut Cuvee $24.00 (3)
Sparkling Wine,'NV, Blanc De Noir Cuvee $15.00 (6)
Sparkling Wine,'NV, Cuvee, Brut Prestige $15.00 (5)

DOMAINE NAPA WINERY
1155 Mee Lane St Helena CA 94574
Chardonnay,'88, Napa Co. $12.50 (3)
Sauvignon Blanc,'88, Napa Vly., Michael A. Penet (3)
Sauvignon Blanc,'89, Napa Vly. $8.50 (3)

DOMAINE ST. GEORGE WINERY
1141 Grant Ave. Healdsburg CA 95448
Cabernet Sauvignon,'86, Select Reserve, Estate (S-Nat'l O.S.)
Cabernet Sauvignon,'87, Alexander Vly., Reserve (S-Orange)
Cabernet Sauvignon,'87, North Coast (B-San Diego)
Sauvignon Blanc,'88, Napa (B-San Diego)
White Zinfandel,'89, California (S-Orange)

DORE
42 Miller Avenue Mill Valley CA 94941
Cabernet Sauvignon,'87, California, Floral Series (B-Orange)
White Zinfandel,'89, California, Floral Series (G-Orange)

DRY CREEK VINEYARD
3770 Lambert Bridge Rd. Healdsburg CA 95448
Cabernet Sauvignon,'87, Sonoma Co. (2)
Chardonnay,'86, Dry Creek Vly. (B-Dallas)
Chardonnay,'87, Dry Creek Vly., Reserve $18.00 (2)
Chardonnay,'88, Sonoma Co. (B-Nat'l O.S.)
Chardonnay,'89, Sonoma Co. $12.50 (4)
Chenin Blanc,'89, California, Dry $6.50 (6)
Meritage Red,'86, Dry Creek Vly., Blende $22.00 (6)
Sauvignon Blanc,'88, Sonoma Co., Fume (B-Dallas)
Sauvignon Blanc,'89, Sonoma Co., Fume $9.25 (4)

DUCKHORN VINEYARDS
3027 Silverado Trail St Helena CA 94574
Cabernet Sauvignon,'87, Napa Vly. (S-Orange)
Sauvignon Blanc,'88, Napa Vly. (S-Dallas)

DUNNEWOOD VINEYARDS
391 Taylor Blvd., #110 Pleasant Hill CA 94523
Cabernet Sauvignon,'86, Napa Vly., Reserve (3)

DURNEY VINEYARD
P.O. Box 222016 Carmel CA 93922
Cabernet Sauvignon,'83, Carmel Vly., Reserve $20.00 (2)

E

EAGLE RIDGE WINERY
111 Goodwin Ave, Penngrove CA 94951
Sparkling Wine,'NV, California, Extra Dry $6.99 (2)
Zinfandel,'NV, Sonoma Coast, LH (2)

EBERLE WINERY
128 Fairview Paso Robles CA 93446
Chardonnay,'87, Paso Robles $12.00 (3)

ELIZABETH VINEYARDS
8591 Colony Drive Redwood Valley CA 95470
Chardonnay,'88, Mendocino (S-Orange)
Sauvignon Blanc,'89, Mendocino $8.00 (B-State Fair)

ESTANCIA
1178 Galleron Rd. Rutherford CA 94573
Cabernet Sauvignon,'87, Alexander Vly. $8.00 (5)
Chardonnay,'88, Monterey $8.00 (2)
Meritage Red,'87, Alexander Vly. (S-W.Coast)

ESTRELLA RIVER WINERY
Shandon Star Rte. Paso Robles CA 93446
Cabernet Sauvignon,'85, Paso Robles $12.00 (2)

F

FALLBROOK WINERY
2608 Via Rancheros Fallbrook CA 92028
Chardonnay,'88, Culbertson Home Vnyd. $13.50 (B-Farmers)

FALLENLEAF VINEYARDS
1075 Buchli Station Rd. Napa CA 94558
Sauvignon Blanc,'88, Sonoma Vly. $8.50 (2)

GARY FARRELL WINES
P. O. Box 342 Forestville CA 95436
Cabernet Sauvignon,'87, Sonoma Co. $16.00 (6)
Chardonnay,'88, Russian River Vly. $16.00 (4)
Pinot Noir,'88, Russian River Vly. $16.00 (4)
Pinot Noir,'88, Russian River Vly., Allen Vnyd. $25.00 (7)
Sauvignon Blanc,'88, Russian River Vly. $8.75 (3)

FARVIEW FARMS
Rt. 2, Box 40 Templeton CA 93465
Cabernet Sauvignon,'86, Paso Robles (B-Orange)

FELTON EMPIRE VINEYARDS
379 Felton Empire Rd. Felton CA 95018
Chardonnay,'88, Monterey Co. (B-San Diego)

FENESTRA CELLARS
83 E. Vallecitos Road Livermore CA 94550
Cabernet Sauvignon,'86, Monterey, Smith & Hook Vnyd. $13.50 (2)
Chardonnay,'88, Monterey, La Riena Vnyd. $12.50 (2)
Merlot,'88, Central Coast $12.50 (3)
Sauvignon Blanc,'88, Livermore Vly. $8.50 (3)

FERRARI-CARANO
8761 Dry Creek Road Healdsburg CA 95448
Merlot,'87, Alexander Vly. (G-Orange)
Sauvignon Blanc,'89, Sonoma Co., Fume (S-Orange)

GLORIA FERRER
23555 Highway 121 Sonoma CA 95476
Sparkling Wine,'85, Sonoma Co. Royal Cuvee $16.00 (7)
Sparkling Wine,'85, Sonoma, Carneros Cuvee $20.00 (6)
Sparkling Wine,'NV, Sonoma Co. Brut $13.00 (5)

FETZER VINEYARDS
1150 Bel Arbes Rd. Redwood Valley CA 95470
Cabernet Sauvignon,'85, Sonoma Co., Reserve $24.00 (5)

Cabernet Sauvignon,'86, Mendocino, Barrel Select $12.00 (7)
Cabernet Sauvignon,'87, California (2)
Chardonnay,'87, Mendocino Co., Reserve (B-Dallas)
Chardonnay,'88, Mendocino Co., Reserve $17.50 (4)
Chardonnay,'88, Mendocino, Barrel Select $12.00 (4)
Chardonnay,'89, California, Sundial $7.49 (3)
Chenin Blanc,'88, California $5.99 (4)
Chenin Blanc,'89, California $5.99 (2)
Gewurztraminer,'89, California $5.99 (5)
Johannisberg Riesling,'88, Sonoma Co., Reserve, LH $10.00 (6)
Johannisberg Riesling,'89, California $6.50 (7)
Pinot Noir,'86, Mendocino Co., Reserve $17.50 (6)
Sauvignon Blanc,'88, California, Valley Oaks Fume $6.49 (2)
White Zinfandel,'89, California $5.99 (4)
Zinfandel,'86, Mendocino Co., Reserve $14.00 (4)
Zinfandel,'88, North Coast, Barrel Select $10.99 (S-State Fair)
Zinfandel,'89, California $5.99 (4)

FIELD STONE WINERY
10075 Highway 128 Healdsburg CA 95448
Cabernet Sauvignon,'85, Alexander Vly., Hoot Owl Creek (2)
Cabernet Sauvignon,'86, Alexander Vly., Estate (B-Orange)
Cabernet Sauvignon,'87, Alexander Vly. (S-W.Coast)
Chardonnay,'88, Sonoma Co. (S-Orange)
Gewurztraminer,'89, Alexander Vly. $7.75 (4)
Johannisberg Riesling,'86, SLH (B-L.A.)
Sauvignon Blanc,'88, Alexander Vly. (B-Orange)

FIELDBROOK VALLEY WINERY
4241 Fieldbrook Rd. Fieldbrook CA 95521
Zinfandel,'89, Mendocino, Pacini Vnyd. $9.50 (G-State Fair)

FILSINGER VINEYARDS
39050 DePortola Rd. Temecula CA 92390
Cabernet Sauvignon,'87, Temecula, Estate (S-Orange)
Chardonnay,'88, Temecula (B-W.Coast)
Chardonnay,'89, Barrel Fermented $8.00 (2)
Sparkling Wine,'NV, California, Extra Dry (S-Orange)
White Zinfandel,'89, Estate (G-Nat'l O.S.)

FIRESTONE VINEYARD
Zaca Station Rd. Los Olivos CA 93441
Cabernet Sauvignon,'87, Santa Ynez Vly. (2)
Chardonnay,'88, Santa Ynez Vly. (B-W.Coast)
Gewurztraminer,'89, Santa Ynez Vly. $7.50 (3)
Johannisberg Riesling,'89, Santa Ynez Vly. $7.50 (3)
Johannisberg Riesling,'89, SLH (S-L.A.)
Merlot,'87, Santa Ynez Vly. (S-Dallas)

FISHER VINEYARDS
6200 St. Helena Rd. Santa Rosa CA 95404
Chardonnay,'88, Napa/Sonoma (S-Orange)

FLORA SPRINGS WINERY
1978 W. Zinfandel Lane St Helena CA 94574
Chardonnay,'88, Napa Vly $15.00 (4)
Chardonnay,'88, Napa Vly, Barrel Ferm. $23.50 (3)
Merlot,'87, Napa Vly., Estate $15.00 (B-State Fair)

THOMAS FOGARTY WINERY
5937 Alpine Road Portola Valley CA 94025
Cabernet Sauvignon,'84, Napa Vly. $15.50 (2)
Chardonnay,'87, Napa Vly., Carneros (B-San Diego)
Gewurztraminer,'89, Monterey Co., Ventana Vnyd. $9.00 (4)
Gewurztraminer,'89, Santa Cruz Mtns., Spring Ridge Vnyd. $9.00 (5)
Pinot Noir,'87, Napa Vly., Carneros $15.00 (5)

FOLIE A DEUX WINERY
3070 St. Helena Highway St Helena CA 94574
Cabernet Sauvignon,'86, Napa Vly. (S-Nat'l O.S.)
Chardonnay,'87, Napa Co. (S-Dallas)
Chardonnay,'88, Napa Vly. $16.00 (4)
Chenin Blanc,'89, Napa Vly. (2)

FOPPIANO WINE COMPANY
12707 Old Redwood Hwy. Healdsburg CA 95448
Cabernet Sauvignon,'88, California $5.25 (B-San Fran)
Petite Sirah,'88, Sonoma Co. $9.50 (3)
Sauvignon Blanc,'87, Russian River Vly. (B-Dallas)

FORTINO WINERY
4525 Hecker Pass Rd. Gilroy CA 95020
Petite Sirah,'84, Central Coast (B-W.Coast)

FOX MOUNTAIN
12707 Old Redwood Hwy. Healdsburg CA 95448
Cabernet Sauvignon,'85, Russian River Vly., Reserve (B-Dallas)

FRANCISCAN OAKVILLE ESTATE
1178 Galleron Rd. Rutherford CA 94573
Cabernet Sauvignon,'85, Napa Vly., Reserve $15.00 (2)
Cabernet Sauvignon,'86, Napa Vly., Library Selection (2)
Cabernet Sauvignon,'87, Alexander Vly. $8.00 (B-San Fran)
Chardonnay,'86, Napa Vly., Reserve (S-San Diego)
Chardonnay,'88, Napa Vly. $12.00 (4)
Chardonnay,'88, Napa Vly., Cuvee Sauvage (2)
Johannisberg Riesling,'88, Reserve, SLH (S-L.A.)
Meritage Red,'86, Napa Vly. Red Table Wine $16.00 (6)
Merlot,'87, Napa Vly. $12.50 (4)
Zinfandel,'88, Napa Vly. $9.00 (2)

FREEMARK ABBEY WINERY
3020 St. Helena Hwy. N. St Helena CA 94574
Cabernet Sauvignon,'86, Napa Vly. (B-Orange)
Chardonnay,'87, Napa Vly (S-Dallas)
Chardonnay,'88, Napa Vly, Carpy Ranch (2)
Johannisberg Riesling,'89, Napa Vly. $8.00 (B-Farmers)
Johannisberg Riesling,'89, Napa, Edelwein Gold, LH $22.00 (2)

FREMONT CREEK
P. O. Box 248 St Helena CA 94574
Cabernet Sauvignon,'86, Mendocino/Napa $9.50 (4)
Chardonnay,'88, Beckstoffer Vnyd. $9.50 (B-Farmers)
Sauvignon Blanc,'88, Beckstoffer Vnyd. $7.50 (B-Farmers)

FRISINGER CELLARS
2277 Dry Creek Road Napa CA 94558
Chardonnay,'88, Napa, Estate $14.00 (3)

FRITZ CELLARS
24691 Dutcher Creek Rd. Cloverdale CA 95425

Chardonnay,'88, Dry Creek Vly. $9.50 (2)
Chardonnay,'88, Russian River Vly. $12.50 (5)
Sauvignon Blanc,'88, Dry Creek Vly. $7.99 (3)

FROG'S LEAP
3358 St. Helena Highway St Helena CA 94574

Chardonnay,'88, Carneros (B-Orange)

G

GAINEY VINEYARD
3950 E. Hwy. 246 Santa Ynez CA 93460

Cabernet Sauvignon,'87, Santa Barbara Co. $13.00 (B-Farmers)
Chardonnay,'88, Santa Barbara Co. (G-Orange)
Johannisberg Riesling,'89, Santa Barbara Co. $7.75 (3)
Pinot Noir,'87, Santa Ynez Vly., Benedict Vnyd. (G-L.A.)
Sauvignon Blanc,'88, Santa Barbara Co. $8.75 (2)

E. & J. GALLO WINERY
P. O. Box 1130 Modesto CA 95353

Gewurztraminer,'86, California, Reserve (B-Orange)
Sauvignon Blanc,'87, California (B-Dallas)
Sauvignon Blanc,'88, California $4.50 (2)
White Zinfandel,'88, California (B-Dallas)
White Zinfandel,'89, California (2)

GAN EDEN WINERY
4950 Ross Road Sebastopol CA 95472

Cabernet Sauvignon,'86, Alexander Vly. (2)
Chardonnay,'88, Sonoma Co./Napa Vly. $12.00 (5)
Chenin Blanc,'87, Alexander Vly., LH (B-L.A.)
Sauvignon Blanc,'88, Sonoma Co., Fume (2)

GARLAND RANCH
8990 Carmel Vly. Rd. Carmel CA 93923

Cabernet Sauvignon,'88, Central Coast (B-Orange)

GAUER ESTATE
18700 Geyserville Ave. Geyserville CA 95441

Chardonnay,'87, Alexander Vly. (B-San Diego)
Chardonnay,'88, Alexander Vly. $16.00 (2)

GEYSER PEAK WINERY
22281 Chianti Rd. Geyserville CA 95441

Cabernet Sauvignon,'86, Alexander Vly., Estate (2)
Cabernet Sauvignon,'87, Sonoma Co. (2)
Chardonnay,'89, Sonoma Co. (S-Orange)
Chenin Blanc,'89, Alexander Vly. $5.95 (2)
Gewurztraminer,'89, California, Soft (2)
Johannisberg Riesling,'89, California, Soft $5.95 (6)
Meritage Red,'86, Alexander Vly., Reserve $18.95 (4)
Merlot,'87, Alexander Vly., Estate (B-Orange)
Merlot,'88, Alexander Vly. (S-Orange)
Sauvignon Blanc,'88, Sonoma Co. $5.95 (2)

GIRARD WINERY
7717 Silverado Trail Oakville CA 94562

Chenin Blanc,'89, Napa Vly., Dry (S-Orange)

GLEN ELLEN WINERY

1883 London Ranch Rd. Glen Ellen CA 95442

Cabernet Sauvignon,'87, California, Proprietors Reserve $5.75 (3)
Chardonnay,'88, Carneros, Sangiacomo, Imagery $16.00 (5)
Chardonnay,'88, Napa Vly., Imagery Series $15.00 (S-State Fair)
Chardonnay,'NV, California, Proprietors Reserve $5.75 (3)
Chenin Blanc,'89, California Proprietor's Reserve $4.50 (3)
Merlot,'87, California, Proprietor's Reserve $6.00 (3)
Petite Sirah,'87, Paso Robles, Imagery Series $14.00 (2)
White Zinfandel,'89, California, Proprietor's Reserve (4)
Zinfandel,'88, Dry Creek, Carreras, Imagery Series $12.00 (6)

GOLD HILL

5660 Vineyard Lane Coloma CA 95613

Chenin Blanc,'89, El Dorado (B-Orange)

GOLDEN CREEK VINEYARD

4480 Wallace Road Santa Rosa CA 95404

Cabernet Sauvignon,'87, Sonoma Co. $10.50 (4)
Merlot,'88, Sonoma Co. $12.00 (4)

GOLDEN STATE VINTNERS

Address not available

Cabernet Sauvignon,'NV, California, Reserve $4.99 (B-State Fair)

GOOSCROSS CELLARS

1119 State Lane Yountville CA 94599

Chardonnay,'87, Napa Vly. (B-Nat'l O.S.)

RICHARD L. GRAESER WINERY

255 Petrified Forest Rd. Calistoga CA 94515

Cabernet Sauvignon,'86, Napa Vly. (2)

GRAHM CREW

Address not available

Chardonnay,'89, California (B-Orange)

GRAND CRU VINEYARDS

1 Vintage Lane Glen Ellen CA 95442

Cabernet Sauvignon,'86, Alexander Vly., Reserve $22.00 (3)
Cabernet Sauvignon,'87, Sonoma Co. $12.00 (3)
Chenin Blanc,'89, Clarksburg, Premium Selection $6.50 (4)
Gewurztraminer,'89, Alexander Vly., Premium Selection $9.00 (4)
Sauvignon Blanc,'88, Sonoma Co., Premium Sel. $9.00 (4)
White Zinfandel,'89, California $6.50 (3)

GRANITE SPRINGS WINERY

6060 Granite Springs Road Somerset CA 95684

Cabernet Sauvignon,'87, El Dorado Co., Estate (2)
Chenin Blanc,'89, El Dorado Co. (B-San Diego)
Petite Sirah,'87, El Dorado, Granite Hill $8.50 (3)
White Zinfandel,'89, El Dorado (G-Orange)
Zinfandel,'87, El Dorado $7.50 (B-San Fran)

GREAT WESTERN WINERY

P. O. Box 780 Gonzales CA 93926

Sparkling Wine,'NV, California Blanc De Noir $8.99 (4)
Sparkling Wine,'NV, California, Blanc De Blanc $8.99 (3)

GREEN & RED VINEYARD
3208 Chiles Pope Vly. Rd. St Helena CA 94574
Chardonnay,'88, Napa Vly., Estate (S-Orange)

GREENSTONE WINERY
Hwy 88 @ Jackson Vly. Rd. Ione CA 95640
Chenin Blanc,'89, Amador Co. (2)

GREENWOOD RIDGE VINEYARDS
24555 Greenwood Road Philo CA 95466
Cabernet Sauvignon,'84, Mendocino Co. (B-W.Coast)
Chardonnay,'89, Mendocino, Lolonis Vnyd. $13.50 (5)
Johannisberg Riesling,'89, Mendocino, Estate $8.00 (5)
Johannisberg Riesling,'89, Mendocino, LH $18.00 (7)
Merlot,'84, Mendocino (B-San Diego)
Sauvignon Blanc,'89, Anderson Vly. $7.50 (5)
Zinfandel,'88, Sonoma Co. $10.75 (4)

GRGICH HILLS CELLAR
1829 St. Helena Highway Rutherford CA 94573
Cabernet Sauvignon,'81, Napa Vly. $20.00 (B-San Diego)
Cabernet Sauvignon,'84, Napa Vly. $20.00 (S-Dallas)
Cabernet Sauvignon,'85, Napa Vly. $20.00 (6)
Chardonnay,'86, Napa Vly. $22.00 (B-San Diego)
Chardonnay,'87, Napa Vly. $22.00 (4)
Chardonnay,'88, Napa Vly. $22.00 (3)
Sauvignon Blanc,'88, Napa Vly., Fume $10.00 (8)
Zinfandel,'85, Alexander Vly. (S-Nat'l O.S.)

GROTH VINEYARDS
750 Oakville Crossroads Oakville CA 94562
Sauvignon Blanc,'88, Napa Vly (B-Dallas)

GUENOC WINERY
21000 Butts Canyon Rd. Middletown CA 95461
Cabernet Sauvignon,'83, Guenoc Vly., Vintner's Sel. (S-Nat'l O.S.)
Cabernet Sauvignon,'85, Guenoc Vly. (S-Dallas)
Cabernet Sauvignon,'85, Guenoc Vly., Premier Cuvee $17.00 (2)
Cabernet Sauvignon,'86, Lake Co. (5)
Chardonnay,'88, Guenoc Vly., Monogram Reserve (3)
Chardonnay,'89, California $7.50 (B-Farmers)
Meritage Red,'87, Langtry, Lake Co./Napa Co. $35.00 (2)
Merlot,'85, Guenoc Vly. (B-Dallas)
Merlot,'86, Napa Co./Lake Co. $12.00 (5)
Petite Sirah,'86, Lake Co. (2)
Petite Sirah,'87, Guenoc Vly. $9.00 (5)
Sauvignon Blanc,'87, Lake Co./Napa Co. $7.50 (2)
Sauvignon Blanc,'88, Lake Co./Napa Co. (2)
Zinfandel,'88, California (B-Orange)

GUGLIELMO WINERY
1480 East Main Ave. Morgan Hill CA 95037
Cabernet Sauvignon,'85, Santa Clara Vly., Reserve $10.00 (2)
Zinfandel,'86, Santa Clara Vly., Reserve $7.50 (2)

GUNDLACH BUNDSCHU WINERY
3775 Thornberry Road Sonoma CA 95476
Cabernet Sauvignon,'86, Sonoma Vly., Rhinefarm Vnyds. $12.00 (6)
Chardonnay,'88, Sonoma Vly. (2)

Chardonnay,'88, Sonoma, Sangiacomo Vnyd. (B-Nat'l O.S.)
Gewurztraminer,'88, Sonoma, Rhinefarm Vnyd. (2)
Gewurztraminer,'89, Sonoma, Rhinefarm, Estate (G-Orange)
Merlot,'87, Sonoma Vly., Rhinefarm Vnyds. $12.00 (5)
Pinot Noir,'88, Sonoma Vly., Rhinefarm Vnyd., Estate $12.00 (5)
Zinfandel,'88, Sonoma Vly., Rhinefarm Vnyds. $8.00 (4)

H

HACIENDA WINERY
1000 Vineyard Lane Sonoma CA 95476
Cabernet Sauvignon,'85, Sonoma Co. $14.00 (5)
Chenin Blanc,'89, Clarksburg $6.50 (6)
Pinot Noir,'87, Sonoma Vly., Estate Reserve (S-Orange)

HAGAFEN CELLARS
P. O. Box 3035 Napa CA 94558
Chardonnay,'89, Napa Vly. (B-Orange)
Johannisberg Riesling,'89, Napa Vly. $8.75 (3)

HALLCREST VINEYARDS
379 Felton Empire Rd. Felton CA 95018
Cabernet Sauvignon,'86, El Dorado, De Cascabel (B-Nat'l O.S.)
Cabernet Sauvignon,'87, El Dorado, De Cascabel $11.00 (2)
Cabernet Sauvignon,'87, Napa Vly., Lyons Vnyd. (B-Dallas)
Chardonnay,'88, California, Fortuyn Cuvee $9.00 (2)
Gewurztraminer,'88, Mendocino Co., Talmage Town (B-Dallas)
Gewurztraminer,'89, Mendocino Co., Talmage Town (S-Orange)

HANDLEY CELLARS
P. O. Box 178 Philo CA 95466
Chardonnay,'87, Anderson Vly. $11.00 (6)
Chardonnay,'88, Dry Creek Vly. $14.50 (5)
Gewurztraminer,'89, Anderson Vly. $7.50 (4)
Sauvignon Blanc,'88, Dry Creek Vly. $8.00 (5)

HANNA WINERY
4345 Occidental Rd. Santa Rosa CA 95401
Cabernet Sauvignon,'87, Sonoma Co. $16.00 (4)
Chardonnay,'87, Sonoma Co. $14.50 (B-Farmers)
Chardonnay,'88, Sonoma Co. (S-Orange)
Sauvignon Blanc,'88, Sonoma Co. (B-San Diego)

HARMONY CELLARS
Address not available
Cabernet Sauvignon,'85, Paso Robles (G-Dallas)
Pinot Noir,'88, Paso Robles $10.00 (B-State Fair)
White Zinfandel,'89, Paso Robles $5.25 (B-State Fair)

HART WINERY
32580 Rancho Calif. Rd. Temecula CA 92390
Merlot,'88, Temecula (S-Orange)
Sauvignon Blanc,'88, Temecula (S-San Diego)
Sauvignon Blanc,'89, Temecula (B-L.A.)

HAVENS WINE CELLARS
1441 Calistoga Avenue Napa CA 94558
Merlot,'87, Napa Vly. $14.00 (B-San Fran)
Merlot,'87, Napa Vly. $20.00 (B-San Fran)

HAYWOOD WINERY
18701 Gehricke Rd. Sonoma CA 95476
Cabernet Sauvignon,'86, Sonoma Vly., Estate (B-San Diego)
Cabernet Sauvignon,'87, Sonoma, Los Chamizal $16.00 (B-State
Chardonnay,'87, Sonoma, Los Chamizal Vnyd. $14.50 (B-San Diego
Chardonnay,'88, Sonoma, Los Chamizal Vnyd. $14.50 (2)
Zinfandel,'88, Sonoma Vly. (2)

BARON HERZOG WINE CELLARS
12378 Saratoga-Sunnyvale Rd. Saratoga CA 95070
Cabernet Sauvignon,'88, California $10.49 (B-Farmers)
Chardonnay,'89, Sonoma Co. (2)
Chenin Blanc,'89, California $4.99 (2)
Gewurztraminer,'89, Sonoma Co., Calif. Selection $7.39 (3)
Johannisberg Riesling,'89, California, LH $7.43 (5)
Sauvignon Blanc,'89, Sonoma Co., Calif. Selection (2)
White Zinfandel,'89, Sonoma Co., Calif. Sel. (S-Orange)

HESS COLLECTION WINERY
4140 Redwood Road Napa CA 94558
Cabernet Sauvignon,'86, Napa Vly. $14.25 (4)
Chardonnay,'88, Napa Vly. $13.75 (8)

HIDDEN CELLARS
1500 Ruddick Cunningham Rd Ukiah CA 95482
Chardonnay,'88, Mendocino Co. $12.00 (5)
Chardonnay,'89, Mendocino Co., Tillman Vnyd. $16.00 (5)
Johannisberg Riesling,'89, Mendocino, Potter Vly. (B-San Diego)
Sauvignon Blanc,'88, Mendocino Co. $8.50 (2)
Zinfandel,'87, Mendocino, Pacini Vnyds. $8.50 (4)

WILLIAM HILL WINERY
1775 Lincoln Ave. Napa CA 94558
Cabernet Sauvignon,'86, Napa Vly., Reserve $24.00 (6)
Chardonnay,'88, Napa Vly., Reserve $18.00 (8)
Johannisberg Riesling,'89, Willamette Vly. $7.50 (3)

HONIG CELLARS
850 Rutherford Road Rutherford CA 94573
Sauvignon Blanc,'88, Napa, Estate $8.75 (S-San Fran)

HOP KILN WINERY
6050 Westside Rd. Healdsburg CA 95448
Cabernet Sauvignon,'86, Dry Creek Vly. $12.00 (3)
Chardonnay,'89, Russian River Vly., M. Griffin Vnyds., Estate (2)
Gewurztraminer,'89, Russian River Vly. (B-Orange)
Petite Sirah,'88, Russian River Vly., Estate $15.00 (B-Farmers)
Zinfandel,'88, Russian River Vly. $12.00 (3)
Zinfandel,'88, Sonoma Co., Primitivo $14.00 (2)

HOUTZ VINEYARDS
2670 Ontiveros Road Los Olivos CA 93441
Chenin Blanc,'88, Santa Ynez Vly. (S-Orange)

HUNTER ASHBY
3022 St. Helena Hwy. N. St Helena CA 95474
Pinot Noir,'86, Napa Vly. (B-Nat'l O.S.)

HUSCH VINEYARDS
P. O. Box 189 Talmage CA 95481

Cabernet Sauvignon,'86, La Ribera Vnyd. $12.00 (B-Nat'l O.S.)
Cabernet Sauvignon,'87, Mendocino, La Ribera $12.00 (5)
Cabernet Sauvignon,'87, Mendocino, North Field (B-Orange)
Chardonnay,'88, Mendocino Co., Estate $11.00 (7)
Chenin Blanc,'89, Mendocino, La Ribera Vnyds. $6.50 (5)
Gewurztraminer,'88, Anderson Vly. $8.00 (B-Dallas)
Gewurztraminer,'89, Anderson Vly., Estate $8.00 (6)
Gewurztraminer,'89, Anderson Vly., Estate, LH $12.00 (2)
Pinot Noir,'87, Anderson Vly. $13.00 (3)
Pinot Noir,'88, Anderson Vly., Estate (S-Orange)
Sauvignon Blanc,'88, Mendocino Co., La Ribera Vnyd. (2)
Sauvignon Blanc,'89, Mendocino Co., La Ribera Vnyd. $8.00 (2)

I

INGLENOOK NAPA VALLEY
100 S. St. Helena Hwy. St Helena CA 94574

Cabernet Sauvignon,'84, Napa, Reserve Cask $15.50 (B-State Fair)
Cabernet Sauvignon,'85, Napa Vly., Estate (S-Orange)
Cabernet Sauvignon,'85, Napa Vly., Reserve Cask $16.00 (3)
Chardonnay,'86, Reserve (B-L.A.)
Chardonnay,'87, Napa Vly., Reserve $15.00 (2)
Chardonnay,'88, Napa Vly., Estate (B-Orange)
Meritage Red,'85, Napa., Reunion $35.00 (3)
Meritage Red,'86, Napa Vly., Niebaum Res. $12.25 (B-Farmers)
Meritage Red,'86, Napa Vly., Reunion $35.00 (2)
Meritage White,'88, Napa Vly., Gravion $9.50 (4)
Merlot,'86, Napa Vly., Reserve $11.25 (6)

IRON HORSE
9786 Ross Station Rd. Sebastopol CA 95472

Sparkling Wine,'87, Green Vly., Blanc De Noir (B-Orange)

J

THOMAS JAEGER WINERY
13455 San Pasqual Rd. Escondido CA 95025
Sauvignon Blanc,'89, San Diego Co. $7.49 (2)

TOBIN JAMES WINERY
P. O. Box 2459 Paso Robles CA 93447

Pinot Noir,'88, Monterey, Le Jus De Soleil (3)
Zinfandel,'88, Paso Robles (4)

JEKEL VINEYARDS
40155 Walnut Avenue Greenfield CA 93927

Chardonnay,'86, Arroyo Seco, Estate $20.00 (2)
Chardonnay,'86, Arroyo Seco, Gravelstone Vnyd. (2)
Johannisberg Riesling,'88, Arroyo Seco, Dry Style $7.50 (2)
Johannisberg Riesling,'88, Arroyo Seco, LH $12.00 (3)
Merlot,'88, Arroyo Seco, Estate $14.50 (S-State Fair)

JEPSON VINEYARDS
10400 S. Highway 101 Ukiah CA 95482

Chardonnay,'87, Mendocino $12.50 (3)
Sauvignon Blanc,'88, Mendocino Co. $7.50 (4)
Sparkling Wine,'85, Mendocino Co., Brut $16.00 (4)

JOANNA VINEYARD
P. O. Box 2318 Yountville CA 94599

Cabernet Sauvignon,'86, Sonoma Co. (B-Orange)

JOHNSON TURNBULL VINEYARDS
8210 St. Helena Hwy. Oakville CA 94562

Cabernet Sauvignon,'87, Napa Vly., Estate (B-Orange)

JORDAN
1474 Alexander Valley Road Healdsburg CA 95448

Cabernet Sauvignon,'86, Alexander Vly., Estate (B-Orange)

JORY WINERY
P.O. Box 1496 Los Gatos CA 95031

Chardonnay,'88, Monterey, La Reina Vnyd., Reserve $22.00 (3)
Chardonnay,'89, Santa Clara Co., Vin Jory (S-Orange)
Pinot Noir,'88, Santa Clara Co., San Ysidro Vnyd. $20.00 (B-Farmers)

JUSTIN VINEYARDS
Address not available

Chardonnay,'88, Paso Robles $13.50 (2)
Meritage Red,'87, Paso Robles, Reserve $15.00 (3)

K

ROBERT KEENAN WINERY
3660 Spring Mtn. Rd. St Helena CA 94574

Cabernet Sauvignon,'87, Napa Vly. (G-Dallas)
Chardonnay,'88, Napa Vly. (B-Dallas)
Merlot,'86, Napa Vly. (S-Dallas)
Merlot,'87, Napa Vly $18.00 (S-State Fair)

KENDALL-JACKSON WINERY
700 Mathews Road Lakeport CA 95453

Cabernet Sauvignon,'86, California, Cardinale $15.00 (5)
Cabernet Sauvignon,'86, California, Proprietor's $24.00 (5)
Cabernet Sauvignon,'86, California, Vintner's Reserve $14.00 (5)
Chardonnay,'88, Anderson Vly. $14.00 (S-San Fran)
Chardonnay,'88, California, The Proprietor's $22.50 (8)
Chardonnay,'89, California, Vintner's Reserve $12.50 (7)
Johannisberg Riesling,'85, Lake Co., SLH $15.00 (2)
Johannisberg Riesling,'89, Clear Lake, Vintner's Reserve $9.00 (7)
Merlot,'87, Sonoma Co., Proprietor's $20.00 (5)
Pinot Noir,'88, Santa Maria Vly., Julia's Vnyd. $15.00 (4)
Sauvignon Blanc,'88, Lake Co., Vintner's Reserve $9.00 (3)
Sauvignon Blanc,'89, Clear Lake, Vintner's Reserve $9.00 (4)
Zinfandel,'86, Mendocino $9.00 (B-San Fran)
Zinfandel,'87, Mendocino Co. (B-Dallas)
Zinfandel,'87, Mendocino Co., Ciapusci Vnyd. (2)
Zinfandel,'88, Mendocino, Vintner's Reserve $10.00 (4)

KENWOOD WINERY
9592 Sonoma Hwy. Kenwood CA 95452

Cabernet Sauvignon,'86, Sonoma Vly. (2)
Cabernet Sauvignon,'87, Sonoma Vly. $12.00 (B-State Fair)
Cabernet Sauvignon,'87, Sonoma, Jack London $18.00 (2)
Chardonnay,'88, Sonoma Vly., Beltane Ranch $13.00 (2)
Chardonnay,'89, Sonoma Vly., Yulupa Vnyd. (B-Orange)
Chenin Blanc,'89, California $6.50 (2)

Johannisberg Riesling,'86, Sonoma Vly., Estate, LH $8.50 (3)
Sauvignon Blanc,'88, Sonoma Co.   (S-San Diego)
Sauvignon Blanc,'89, Sonoma $9.50 (2)
Zinfandel,'87, Sonoma Vly.   (S-W.Coast)
Zinfandel,'87, Sonoma Vly., Jack London Vnyd. $12.00 (2)
Zinfandel,'88, Sonoma Vly., Jack London $14.00 (G-State Fair)

ONOCTI WINERY

Hwy. 29 & Thomas Kelseyville CA 95451

Cabernet Sauvignon,'86, Lake Co.   (B-San Diego)
Cabernet Sauvignon,'89, Kah-Nock-Tie, Spring Rel.   (B-L.A.)
Chardonnay,'88, Lake Co. $9.00 (5)
Chardonnay,'89, Kah-Nock-Tie, Spring Release   (B-Orange)
Johannisberg Riesling,'86, Lake Co., LH $10.00 (2)
Johannisberg Riesling,'89, Lake Co. $7.50 (4)
Meritage Red,'87, Lake Co., Estate Reserve $17.00 (2)
Meritage White,'88, Clear Lake, Meritage, Estate $14.00 (7)
Merlot,'87, Lake Co.   (B-W.Coast)
Sauvignon Blanc,'89, Lake Co. $7.50 (5)

ORBEL

13250 River Road Forestville CA 95446

Sparkling Wine,'NV, California Brut   (B-W.Coast)
Sparkling Wine,'NV, California, Blanc De Blanc   (3)
Sparkling Wine,'NV, California, Blanc De Noir $12.50 (4)
Sparkling Wine,'NV, California, Brut Rose $10.50 (3)
Sparkling Wine,'NV, California, Extra Dry $10.50 (3)
Sparkling Wine,'NV, California, Natural $12.50 (6)

ANS KORNELL WINERY

1091 Larkmead Lane St Helena CA 94574

Sparkling Wine,'84, Muscat Alexandria   (B-L.A.)
Sparkling Wine,'NV, Brut Champagne   (B-L.A.)

HARLES KRUG WINERY

200 Main Street St Helena CA 95474

Cabernet Sauvignon,'83, Napa Vly., Vintage Selection $20.00 (2)
Cabernet Sauvignon,'84, Napa Vly., Vintage Selection $20.00 (4)
Cabernet Sauvignon,'85, Napa Vly. $10.50 (4)

L

A BELLE CELLARS

849 Zinfandel Lane St Helena CA 95474

Chardonnay,'88, California $5.75 (B-State Fair)

A CRESTA/MASSON

800 So. Alta Street Saratoga CA 95070

Sparkling Wine,'NV, California, Brut   (B-Dallas)
Sparkling Wine,'NV, California, Extra Dry   (B-Nat'l O.S.)

A REINA WINERY

P. O. Box 1010 Gonzales CA 93936

Chardonnay,'87, Monterey $13.50 (2)

AKE SONOMA WINERY

P. O. Box 263 Healdsburg CA 95448

Cabernet Sauvignon,'86, Dry Creek Vly. $14.00 (S-State Fair)

LAKESPRING WINERY
2055 Hoffman Lane Napa CA 94558

Merlot,'87, Napa Vly. $14.00 (S-State Fair)
Sauvignon Blanc,'89, Napa Vly., Yountmill Vnyd.   (G-Orange)

LAMBERT BRIDGE
4085 W. Dry Creek Rd. Healdsburg CA 95448

Cabernet Sauvignon,'87, Dry Creek Vly.   (B-Dallas)
Cabernet Sauvignon,'87, Dry Creek Vly., Library Reserve $15.00 (3)
Chardonnay,'87, Dry Creek Vly. (2)
Chardonnay,'87, Sonoma Co. $14.00 (B-State Fair)
Chardonnay,'88, Dry Creek Vly., Tete De Cuvee $22.00 (2)
Chardonnay,'88, Sonoma Co. (S-Orange)
Merlot,'88, Sonoma $16.00 (3)
Sauvignon Blanc,'88, Dry Creek Vly., Fume $10.00 (2)

LANDMARK VINEYARDS
9150 Los Amigos Rd Windsor CA 95492

Chardonnay,'87, Sonoma Co.   (4)

LANG WINES
Address not available

Zinfandel,'87, El Dorado, Twin Rivers Vnyd. $8.50 (B-State Fair)

LAS VINAS WINERY
5573 Woodbridge Rd. Lodi CA 95242

Cabernet Sauvignon,'87, Lodi   (B-Dallas)
Zinfandel,'87, Lodi   (S-Dallas)

LAURA'S VINEYARD
Shandon Star Rte. Paso Robles CA 93447

Cabernet Sauvignon,'85, Paso Robles   (B-W.Coast)
Chardonnay,'87, Paso Robles   (B-San Diego)

LAVA CAP WINERY
2221 Fruitridge Rd. Placerville CA 95667

Chardonnay,'88, El Dorado Co.   (B-Dallas)
Sauvignon Blanc,'88, El Dorado   (S-W.Coast)
White Zinfandel,'89, El Dorado   (B-Nat'l O.S.)

LEEWARD WINERY
2784 Johnson Dr. Ventura CA 93003

Cabernet Sauvignon,'86, Alexander Vly.   (2)
Cabernet Sauvignon,'87, Alexander Vly.   (B-W.Coast)
Chardonnay,'89, Central Coast $11.00 (5)

LIBERTY SCHOOL
8700 Conn Creek Rd. Rutherford CA 94573

Chardonnay,'89, California, Lot 18   (G-Orange)

LLORDS & ELWOOD WINERY
6525 Washington St. Yountville CA 94599

Cabernet Sauvignon,'83, Napa Vly. (S-San Diego)
Chardonnay,'88, Napa Vly., The Rare (G-Orange)

J. LOHR WINERY
1000 Lenzen Ave. San Jose CA 95126

Cabernet Sauvignon,'85, Napa Vly. (B-W.Coast)
Cabernet Sauvignon,'85, Napa Vly., Carol's Vnyd., Lot 2 (2)
Cabernet Sauvignon,'85, Napa, Carol's Vnyd., Reserve $17.50 (2)
Cabernet Sauvignon,'87, California (3)

Chardonnay,'88, Monterey Co., Riverstone $12.00 (3)
Johannisberg Riesling,'89, Monterey Co. LH $9.00 (8)
Johannisberg Riesling,'89, Monterey, Greenfield $6.00 (4)
White Zinfandel,'88, California (B-San Diego)

)LONIS WINERY
2901 Road B Redwood Valley CA 95470
Cabernet Sauvignon,'86, Mendocino, Private Reserve $15.00 (5)
Chardonnay,'88, Mendocino Co., Reserve $18.00 (6)
Zinfandel,'88, Mendocino, Reserve $10.00 (S-Farmers)

'ETH WINERY
24625 Chianti Rd. Geyserville CA 95441
Meritage Red,'85, Alexander Vly. $22.50 (G-San Fran)
Meritage Red,'86, Alexander Vly. $22.50 (3)

'NFRED WINERY
Address not available
Chenin Blanc,'NV, California, Reserve (B-Orange)
Johannisberg Riesling,'NV, California, Reserve (B-Orange)

'TTON SPRINGS WINERY
650 Lytton Springs Rd. Healdsburg CA 95448
Cabernet Sauvignon,'87, Mendocino Co., Reserve (2)
Zinfandel,'87, Sonoma Co. (B-Dallas)
Zinfandel,'88, Sonoma Co. $12.00 (3)

M

MARION & COMPANY
5350 Skylane Blvd. #201 Santa Rosa CA 95403
Pinot Noir,'88, California (2)

AACAMA CREEK
Address not available
Cabernet Sauvignon,'88, Alexander Vly., Estate (S-Orange)

ACROSTIE WINERY
17246 Woodland Ave. Sonoma CA 95476
Chardonnay,'88, Carneros (B-San Diego)

ADDALENA VINEYARD
737 Lamar Street Los Angeles CA 90031
Chardonnay,'88, Napa Vly. (B-Orange)
Johannisberg Riesling,'89, Central Coast $5.00 (G-Farmers)
Merlot,'87, Central Coast (S-San Diego)

ADRONA VINEYARDS
P. O. Box 454, Gatlin Rd. Camino CA 95709
Cabernet Sauvignon,'82, El Dorado, Estate $9.50 (B-State Fair)
Merlot,'85, El Dorado, Estate $10.00 (2)
White Zinfandel,'89, El Dorado $5.25 (2)

AGNUS
Address not available
Meritage Red,'86, Ventana Vnyd. (S-Orange)

AISON DEUTZ WINERY
453 Deutz Dr. Arroyo Grande CA 93420
Sparkling Wine,'NV, S. Barbara/SLO, Brut Cuvee $17.00 (6)
Sparkling Wine,'NV, Santa Barbara/SLO, Rose $21.00 (5)

MANZANITA RIDGE
Address not available
Chardonnay,'88, Sonoma $10.00 (B-San Fran)

MARIO PERELLI-MINETTI
1443 Silverado Trail St Helena CA 94574
Cabernet Sauvignon,'85, Napa Vly. (B-Orange)
Chardonnay,'88, Napa Vly. (2)

MARK WEST VINEYARDS
7000 Trenton-Healdsburg Rd. Forestville CA 95436
Chardonnay,'87, Russian River Vly., Le Beau Vnyds. $12.00 (2)
Johannisberg Riesling,'87, Russian River Vly., Estate $7.50 (2)
Pinot Noir,'86, Russian River Vly., Ellis Vnyd. $14.00 (2)
Sparkling Wine,'84, Blanc De Noir $16.50 (2)
Zinfandel,'86, Sonoma Co., Robert Rue Vnyd. (B-San Diego)

MARKHAM VINEYARDS
2812 N. St. Helena Hwy. St Helena CA 94574
Cabernet Sauvignon,'85, Napa Vly $13.50 (6)
Chardonnay,'88, Napa Vly. (B-San Diego)
Merlot,'87, Napa Vly. $13.50 (8)
Sauvignon Blanc,'89, Napa Vly. $7.00 (6)

MARTIN BROTHERS WINERY
P. O. Box 2597 Paso Robles CA 93447
Cabernet Sauvignon,'87, Paso Robles (B-San Diego)
Chardonnay,'89, Paso Robles, Estate $10.00 (2)
Chenin Blanc,'89, Paso Robles, Estate (2)
White Zinfandel,'89, Paso Robles (S-Orange)
Zinfandel,'87, Paso Robles (B-Dallas)

MARTINELLI VINEYARDS
3360 River Road Windsor CA 95436
Sauvignon Blanc,'88, Russian River Vly. $7.25 (B-State Fair)

LOUIS M. MARTINI
St. Helena Hwy. St Helena CA 94574
Cabernet Sauvignon,'86, Vineyard Select (B-Nat'l O.S.)
Cabernet Sauvignon,'87, Napa Vly., Reserve $12.99 (4)
Cabernet Sauvignon,'87, Sonoma Co. $9.45 (3)
Cabernet Sauvignon,'NV, Napa Vly., Reserve (S-L.A.)
Chardonnay,'88, Napa Co./Sonoma Co. $9.45 (B-Farmers)
Gewurztraminer,'88, Russian River Vly. $7.05 (B-Farmers)
Johannisberg Riesling,'88, Sonoma Vly. $7.05 (B-Farmers)
Merlot,'87, North Coast (2)
Merlot,'87, Russian River Vly., Los Vinedos Del Rio (3)
Petite Sirah,'86, Napa Vly. (B-San Diego)
Pinot Noir,'82, Napa Vly., La Loma, Vintage Sel. (B-San Diego)
Pinot Noir,'87, Napa Vly. (B-San Diego)
Sauvignon Blanc,'89, Napa Vly. $6.99 (3)

PAUL MASSON VINEYARDS
13150 Saratoga Avenue Saratoga CA 95070
Cabernet Sauvignon,'86, Monterey Co. $8.00 (4)
Chardonnay,'88, Monterey Co., Vintage Selection (B-Orange)
Chenin Blanc,'89, California, Premium (S-Orange)
Johannisberg Riesling,'88, Monterey Co., Arroyo Seco (3)
Merlot,'87, Monterey Co. $8.00 (4)

Sauvignon Blanc,'88, California, Vintner Sel. (S-San Diego)
Sparkling Wine,'86, Monterey, Grand Cuvee (3)
Sparkling Wine,'NV, California, Extra Dry (2)
White Zinfandel,'89, California, Vintners Sel. (S-Orange)
Zinfandel,'86, California, Vintners Sel. (B-San Diego)

MATANZAS CREEK WINERY
6097 Bennett Vly. Rd. Santa Rosa CA 95404
Chardonnay,'88, Sonoma Co. (S-Orange)
Merlot,'87, Sonoma Co. (B-Orange)
Sauvignon Blanc,'88, Sonoma Co. (G-Orange)

MAYACAMAS VINEYARDS
1155 Lokoya Rd. Napa CA 94558
Chardonnay,'87, Napa Vly. (B-San Diego)
Zinfandel,'84, Napa Vly., LH (G-Orange)

MAZZOCCO VINEYARDS
1400 Lytton Springs Rd. Healdsburg CA 95448
Cabernet Sauvignon,'87, Alexander Vly. $20.00 (2)
Chardonnay,'87, Alexander Vly. (B-Dallas)
Chardonnay,'88, Alexander Vly. $16.50 (4)
Zinfandel,'88, Sonoma Co. $13.00 (2)

MC DOWELL VALLEY VINEYARDS
3811 Highway 175 Hopland CA 95449
Cabernet Sauvignon,'87, California $8.95 (B-Farmers)
Cabernet Sauvignon,'87, Mendocino Co., Reserve (B-San Diego)
Chardonnay,'88, California (B-Orange)
Sauvignon Blanc,'88, Mendocino Fume $7.50 (B-State Fair)
Zinfandel,'87, Mc Dowell Vly., Estate (B-Dallas)
Zinfandel,'88, Mc Dowell Vly. $9.50 (2)

MELIM VINEYARDS
15001 Chalk Hill Rd. Healdsburg CA 95448
Cabernet Sauvignon,'87, Alexander Vly., Reserve (G-Dallas)
Chardonnay,'89, Sonoma, Maacama Creek $8.00 (B-State Fair)

MERIDIAN VINEYARDS
2000 Main Street St Helena CA 94574
Chardonnay,'88, Santa Barbara Co. $9.00 (5)

MERLION WINERY
880 Vallejo St. Napa CA 94559
Meritage White,'86, Napa Vly. (B-W.Coast)

MERRYVALE VINEYARDS
3640 Buchanan Street San Francisco CA 94123
Meritage Red,'86, Napa Vly. (2)

MICHTOM VINEYARDS
1440 Grove St. Healdsburg CA 95448
Cabernet Sauvignon,'85, Alexander Vly. (B-Orange)

MILAT VINEYARDS
1091 S. St. Helena Hwy. St Helena CA 94574
Chardonnay,'89, Napa Vly. (B-San Diego)
Chenin Blanc,'89, Napa Vly. $6.50 (3)

MILL CREEK VINEYARDS
1401 Westside Rd. Healdsburg CA 95448
Merlot,'86, Dry Creek Vly., Estate $9.00 (2)

Sauvignon Blanc,'87, Dry Creek Vly., Estate (S-San Diego)

MIRASSOU VINEYARDS
3000 Aborn Rd. San Jose CA 95135

Cabernet Sauvignon,'85, Napa Vly., Fifth Generation Reserve (2)
Cabernet Sauvignon,'86, California, Fifth Generation Sel. $9.00 (2)
Chardonnay,'88, Monterey, Fifth Generation Reserve (2)
Chenin Blanc,'88, Monterey Co., Family Sel. $6.00 (S-Farmers)
Johannisberg Riesling,'87, Monterey, LH $10.00 (S-Farmers)
Petite Sirah,'87, Monterey Co., Family Sel. $7.00 (3)
Pinot Noir,'86, Monterey, Harvest Reserve $12.00 (B-Farmers)
Sparkling Wine,'83, Monterey (S-W.Coast)
Sparkling Wine,'83, Monterey, Brut Reserve (G-L.A.)
Sparkling Wine,'84, Monterey, Au Naturel (B-L.A.)
Sparkling Wine,'84, Monterey, Brut (S-L.A.)
Sparkling Wine,'84, Monterey, Fifth Gen. Cuvee (2)
White Zinfandel,'89, Pastel (S-L.A.)
Zinfandel,'85, California (2)
Zinfandel,'86, Santa Clara Vly., Reserve (S-San Diego)

MISSION VIEW VINEYARDS
P. O. Box 129 San Miguel CA 93451

Chardonnay,'88, Paso Robles, Estate $9.50 (3)
Chardonnay,'89, Paso Robles, Estate $9.50 (2)
Sauvignon Blanc,'89, San Luis Obispo, Estate $8.50 (B-State Fair)
Zinfandel,'86, Paso Robles $8.00 (3)

C. K. MONDAVI
2800 Main St. St Helena CA 94574

Zinfandel,'NV, California (B-Orange)

ROBERT MONDAVI WINERY
7801 St. Helena Hwy. Oakville CA 94562

Cabernet Sauvignon,'86, Napa Vly., Reserve (2)
Cabernet Sauvignon,'87, Napa, Unfiltered, Res. (B-San Diego)
Chardonnay,'87, Napa Vly., Reserve $26.00 (G-San Diego)
Chardonnay,'88, Napa Vly, Reserve $26.00 (B-San Fran)
Chardonnay,'88, Napa Vly. $16.00 (2)
Pinot Noir,'87, Napa Vly., Reserve (2)
Pinot Noir,'88, Napa Vly. (2)
Sauvignon Blanc,'83, Napa Vly., Botrytis (G-Orange)
Sauvignon Blanc,'88, California (B-Dallas)
Sauvignon Blanc,'88, Napa Vly., Fume, Reserve $15.00 (2)

MONT ST. JOHN CELLARS
5400 Old Sonoma Rd. Napa CA 94558

Cabernet Sauvignon,'84, Napa Vly. $14.00 (2)
Cabernet Sauvignon,'85, Napa Vly. $14.00 (7)
Chardonnay,'88, Napa Vly., Carneros, Estate $12.75 (2)
Pinot Noir,'87, Napa Vly., Carneros (B-Dallas)
Pinot Noir,'88, Napa Vly., Estate (B-San Diego)

MONTE VERDE WINERY
P. O. Box 1287 Paso Robles CA 93447

Cabernet Sauvignon,'88, Paso Robles,Reserve $6.50 (B-State Fair)
Chardonnay,'89, California, Proprietor's Reserve (B-San Diego)

MONTEREY PENINSULA WINERY
2999 Monterey-Salinas Hwy. Monterey CA 93940

Cabernet Sauvignon,'84, Monterey, Doctor's Reserve $16.00 (4)

Merlot,'86, Monterey, Doctors' Reserve $16.00 (S-State Fair)
Pinot Noir,'87, Monterey $18.00 (B-San Fran)
Zinfandel,'80, California, LH $7.50 (B-Farmers)

MONTEREY VINEYARD
800 So. Alta St. Gonzales CA 93926

Cabernet Sauvignon,'86, Monterey Co., Classic (S-Nat'l O.S.)
Cabernet Sauvignon,'86, Monterey Co., Ltd. Release (2)
Cabernet Sauvignon,'87, Monterey Co. (B-W.Coast)
Chardonnay,'87, Monterey Co. (B-W.Coast)
Chardonnay,'87, Monterey Co., Ltd. Release (B-San Diego)
Chardonnay,'88, Monterey Co., Classic (G-Nat'l O.S.)
Chardonnay,'89, Central Coast Classic $5.50 (B-Farmers)
Chenin Blanc,'89, Monterey Co., Classic (B-L.A.)
Sauvignon Blanc,'88, Monterey Co., Classic (B-San Diego)

MONTEVINA VINEYARDS
20680 Shenandoah School Road Plymouth CA 95669

Cabernet Sauvignon,'87, California (S-Orange)
Chardonnay,'88, California $8.00 (B-Farmers)
Sauvignon Blanc,'88, California, Fume $5.75 (2)
Zinfandel,'87, Amador Co. (B-Dallas)

MONTICELLO CELLARS
4242 Big Ranch Rd. Napa CA 94558

Cabernet Sauvignon,'87, Napa Vly., Jefferson Cuvee $14.00 (5)

MONTPELLIER VINEYARDS
P. O. Box 789 Ceres CA 95307

Cabernet Sauvignon,'88, California $8.00 (S-San Fran)
White Zinfandel,'89, California $5.00 (2)

MORGAN WINERY
526-E Brunken Ave. Salinas CA 93901

Cabernet Sauvignon,'87, Carmel Vly. (G-Orange)
Chardonnay,'88, Monterey, Reserve (S-Orange)
Pinot Noir,'87, California (B-Dallas)

J. W. MORRIS WINERY
101 Grant Ave. Healdsburg CA 95448

Cabernet Sauvignon,'88, California, Reserve (S-Orange)
White Zinfandel,'89, California, Reserve (B-Orange)

MOSBY WINERY
Address not available

Pinot Noir,'86, Santa Barbara Co. (B-San Diego)

MOUNT EDEN VINEYARDS
22020 Mt. Eden Road Saratoga CA 95070

Chardonnay,'88, Edna Vly., MacGregor Vnyd. (S-Orange)

MOUNT PALOMAR WINERY
33820 Rancho Calif. Rd. Temecula CA 92390

Cabernet Sauvignon,'85, Dry Creek Vly. $10.00 (3)
Chenin Blanc,'89, Temecula $6.00 (3)
Johannisberg Riesling,'89, Temecula (2)

MOUNT VEEDER WINERY
1999 Mt. Veeded Rd. Napa CA 94558

Cabernet Sauvignon,'86, Napa Vly., Mt. Veeder Vnyd. $18.00 (2)
Cabernet Sauvignon,'87, Napa Vly $18.50 (B-San Fran)

Chardonnay,'87, Napa Vly. (B-W.Coast)
Chardonnay,'88, Napa Vly. $16.00 (5)

MOUNTAIN VIEW VINTNERS

2263 Old Middlefield Mountain View CA 94043

Pinot Noir,'88, Monterey Co. (B-Orange)

MURPHY-GOODE WINERY

3740 Hwy. 128 Geyserville CA 95441

Cabernet Sauvignon,'87, Alexander Vly., Premier Vnyd. $16.50 (3)
Chardonnay,'89, Alexander Vly. $12.00 (2)
Merlot,'88, Alexander Vly., Estate $16.00 (B-State Fair)
Sauvignon Blanc,'88, Alexander Vly. $8.50 (4)

N

NAPA CREEK WINERY

1001 Silverado Trail St Helena CA 94574

Chardonnay,'88, Napa Vly. $15.00 (2)
Merlot,'87, Napa Vly. (3)

NAPA PRIVATE CELLAR

3103 Silverado Trail Napa CA 94558

Chardonnay,'88, Napa Vly. (S-Orange)

NAPA RIDGE WINERY

2000 Main Street St Helena CA 94574

Cabernet Sauvignon,'87, North Coast (2)
Chardonnay,'89, Central Coast (2)
Chenin Blanc,'89, Central Coast $5.25 (2)
Gewurztraminer,'89, Central Coast $5.25 (4)
White Zinfandel,'89, Lodi $5.25 (4)

NAVALLE SELECTIONS

1991 St. Helena Hwy. Rutherford CA 94573

Sauvignon Blanc,'87, California (B-Orange)
White Zinfandel,'89, California $4.99 (2)

NAVARRO VINEYARDS

5601 Highway 128 Philo CA 95466

Cabernet Sauvignon,'85, Mendocino $14.00 (3)
Chardonnay,'88, Anderson Vly., Reserve $14.00 (4)
Chardonnay,'88, Anderson Vly., Table Wine $7.00 (G-State Fair)
Chardonnay,'88, Mendocino $9.75 (6)
Gewurztraminer,'88, Anderson Vly. $8.50 (7)
Johannisberg Riesling,'86, Anderson Vly., LH $25.00 (4)
Johannisberg Riesling,'88, Anderson Vly., LH $12.00 (B-Farmers)
Johannisberg Riesling,'89, Anderson Vly. (S-San Diego)
Pinot Noir,'87, Anderson Vly., Reserve $14.00 (4)

NEVADA CITY WINERY

321 Spring St. Nevada City CA 95959

Cabernet Sauvignon,'87, Sierra Foothills (2)
Gewurztraminer,'89, Sonoma Co. $7.00 (4)
Merlot,'87, Sierra Foothills (2)
Pinot Noir,'88, Nevada Co. $8.00 (2)
Zinfandel,'88, Sierra Foothills $7.50 (B-Farmers)

NEVADA COUNTY WINE GUILD

Address not available

Chardonnay,'89, Nevada Co., Jewett Vnyd. (G-Orange)

Petite Sirah,'88, Sierra Foothills   (G-Orange)

NEWLAN VINEYARDS
1305 Carrell Lane Napa CA 94558
Chardonnay,'88, Napa $14.00 (S-San Fran)
Johannisberg Riesling,'89, Napa Vly., LH   (B-L.A.)
Pinot Noir,'87, Napa Vly., Estate   (2)

NEWTON VINEYARD
2555 Madrona Ave. St Helena CA 94573
Cabernet Sauvignon,'86, Napa Vly.   (G-Orange)
Chardonnay,'88, Napa Vly. $14.00 (4)
Merlot,'86, Napa Vly. $15.85 (2)
Merlot,'87, Napa Vly. $16.75 (2)

GUSTAVE NIEBAUM COLLECTION
Address not available
Cabernet Sauvignon,'86, Napa Vly., Tench Vnyd. $14.00 (2)
Chardonnay,'88, Napa Vly., Carneros, Laird Vnyd. $14.00 (3)
Meritage White,'88, Napa Vly., Herrick Vnyd. $11.00 (S-State Fair)

O

OBESTER WINERY
12341 San Mateo Rd. Half Moon Bay CA 94019
Chardonnay,'88, Mendocino Co. $13.00 (B-State Fair)
Gewurztraminer,'89, Anderson Vly. $7.00 (2)
Johannisberg Riesling,'89, Monterey Co., Ventana Vnyd. $7.00 (3)
Sauvignon Blanc,'89, Mendocino Co. $8.50 (2)

OLD CREEK RANCH WINERY
10024 Old Creek Rd. Oakview CA 93022
Merlot,'87, Santa Maria Vly., Rancho Sisquoc Vnyd.   (B-Orange)

ED OLIVEIRA WINERY
156 Center Ave. Arcata CA 95521
Cabernet Sauvignon,'86, Knights Vly. $12.00 (2)

OLIVET LANE ESTATE
Address not available
Chardonnay,'88, Russian River Vly.   (B-W.Coast)

OLSON WINERY
3620 Road B Redwood Valley CA 95474
Cabernet Sauvignon,'86, Mendocino Co. $10.00 (3)
Chardonnay,'89,   (S-L.A.)
Petite Sirah,'87, Mendocino Co. $7.99 (B-Farmers)
Sauvignon Blanc,'89, Mendocino Co., Fume $7.99 (S-Farmers)
Zinfandel,'87, Mendocino Co.   (3)

OPUS ONE
7801 St. Helena Hwy. Oakville CA 94562
Meritage Red,'86, Napa Vly.   (S-Orange)

P

PAGE MILL WINERY
13686 Page Mill Rd. Los Altos Hills CA 94022
Cabernet Sauvignon,'85, Napa, Volker Eisele Vnyd. $13.50 (B-State
Pinot Noir,'88, Santa Barbara, Bien Nacido Vnyd.   (S-L.A.)
Zinfandel,'86, Napa $10.00 (B-San Fran)

PAGOR

Address not available

Pinot Noir,'88, Santa Barbara Co. (B-Orange)

PALISADES VINEYARDS

Address not available

Cabernet Sauvignon,'86, Napa Vly., Reserve $9.00 (3)

PARDUCCI WINE CELLARS

501 Parducci Rd. Ukiah CA 95482

Cabernet Sauvignon,'87, North Coast $9.59 (B-State Fair)
Chardonnay,'86, Mendocino $9.50 (B-San Fran)
Chardonnay,'88, North Coast, Cellarmaster (G-L.A.)
Chardonnay,'89, Mendocino Co. $9.50 (B-State Fair)
Chenin Blanc,'88, Mendocino Co. $6.49 (2)
Chenin Blanc,'89, Mendocino Co. $4.50 (4)
Gewurztraminer,'88, Mendocino Co. (2)
Gewurztraminer,'89, Mendocino (B-L.A.)
Johannisberg Riesling,'89, Mendocino Co. $6.50 (2)
Meritage Red,'86, Mendocino Co., Cabernet/Merlot (2)
Merlot,'86, North Coast (S-San Diego)
Merlot,'87, North Coast $9.50 (2)
Petite Sirah,'80, Mendocino Co., Cellarmaster Select. (B-Dallas)
Petite Sirah,'86, Mendocino Co. $6.50 (2)
Pinot Noir,'87, Mendocino Co. $12.00 (3)
Sauvignon Blanc,'88, Mendocino, Cellarmaster Sel. (S-Orange)
Sauvignon Blanc,'88, North Coast $7.49 (5)
White Zinfandel,'89, California $5.99 (2)
Zinfandel,'84, Mendocino, LH $12.00 (B-Farmers)
Zinfandel,'87, North Coast $6.49 (2)

PARSONS CREEK WINERY

3001 S. State St. Ukiah CA 95482

Cabernet Sauvignon,'86, Alexander Vly. (B-Orange)
Chardonnay,'87, Sonoma Co., Carneros $8.50 (3)
Chardonnay,'88, Sonoma $8.00 (B-San Fran)
Chardonnay,'88, Sonoma Co., Winemakers Select $13.00 (4)
Sparkling Wine,'NV, Sonoma Co., Brut $13.00 (2)
Sparkling Wine,'NV, Sonoma, Tete De Cuvee $12.00 (3)

PAT PAULSEN VINEYARDS

25510 River Rd. Cloverdale CA 95425

Cabernet Sauvignon,'85, Sonoma Co. (2)

ROBERT PECOTA WINERY

3299 Bennett Lane Calistoga CA 94515

Cabernet Sauvignon,'87, Napa Vly., Kara's Vnyd. $16.00 (4)

J PEDRONCELLI WINERY

1220 Canyon Road Geyserville CA 95441

Cabernet Sauvignon,'82, Dry Creek Vly., Reserve (3)
Cabernet Sauvignon,'85, Dry Creek Vly., Reserve (B-San Diego)
Chenin Blanc,'88, Alexander Vly. $5.50 (B-State Fair)
Chenin Blanc,'89, Alexander Vly $5.50 (G-San Fran)
Johannisberg Riesling,'86, LH (S-L.A.)
Pinot Noir,'86, Dry Creek Vly. $7.50 (B-Farmers)
Sauvignon Blanc,'89, Sonoma Co., Fume (B-Orange)

PEJU PROVINCE WINERY

8466 St. Helena Highway Rutherford CA 94573

Cabernet Sauvignon,'87, Napa Vly., HB Vnyd. $20.00 (3)
Chardonnay,'89, Napa Vly., LH $12.50 (B-State Fair)

PELLEGRINI VINEYARDS

272 So. Maple Ave. So San Francisco CA 94080

Chardonnay,'88, Russian River Vly. $9.75 (B-State Fair)
Pinot Noir,'88, Russian River Vly., Olivet Lane $11.75 (B-Farmers)

ROBERT PEPI

7585 St. Helena Hwy. Oakville CA 94562

Cabernet Sauvignon,'86, Napa Vly. $19.00 (B-San Fran)
Chardonnay,'88, Napa Vly. $15.00 (3)
Sauvignon Blanc,'86, Calif., Dolcezza D'Oro $20.00 (S-San Fran)
Sauvignon Blanc,'89, Napa Vly. $10.00 (B-San Fran)

PESENTI WINERY

2900 Vineyard Drive Templeton CA 93465

Cabernet Sauvignon,'88, Paso Robles, Family Reserve $10.00 (2)
Sauvignon Blanc,'NV, San Luis Obispo Co. (S-L.A.)
White Zinfandel,'NV, San Luis Obispo Co. $5.00 (B-Farmers)
Zinfandel,'82, Reserve, LH Dry $6.00 (B-Farmers)

JOSEPH PHELPS VINEYARDS

1230-A Churchill Downs Woodland CA 94695

Chardonnay,'89, California $7.00 (2)
Chenin Blanc,'88, Dunnigan Hills Vnyd., Dry $3.99 (B-Farmers)
Johannisberg Riesling,'87, Napa Vly., LH (S-Orange)
White Zinfandel,'89, California, Night Harvest $5.00 (2)

R. H. PHILLIPS VINEYARD

Route 1, Box 855 Esparto CA 95627

Chardonnay,'89, California (S-L.A.)
Chenin Blanc,'89, Yolo Co., Dunnigan Hills Vnyd. $3.00 (2)

JOHN PICONI WINERY

33410 Rancho California Rd. Temecula CA 92390

Johannisberg Riesling,'89, Temecula (B-San Diego)

PINE RIDGE

5901 Silverado Trail Napa CA 94558

Cabernet Sauvignon,'86, Napa Vly., Stags Leap (B-Orange)
Merlot,'87, Napa Vly., Selected Cuvee (B-Orange)

PIPER SONOMA

11447 Old Redwood Highway Healdsburg CA 95448

Sparkling Wine,'86, Sonoma, Blanc De Noir (G-Orange)

PLAM VINEYARDS

6200 St. Helena Hwy. Napa CA 94558

Cabernet Sauvignon,'87, Napa Vly. (S-Orange)
Chardonnay,'88, Napa Vly. (S-Orange)

POPPY HILL CELLARS

5400 Old Sonoma Rd. Napa CA 94559

Cabernet Sauvignon,'86, California $6.99 (2)
Zinfandel,'86, Napa Vly. (B-San Diego)

PORTER CREEK VINEYARDS
8735 Westside Road Healdsburg CA 95448
Pinot Noir,'87, Russian River Vly. $10.50 (B-Farmers)
Pinot Noir,'88, Russian River Vly., Hillside Vynd. $20.00 (B-State Fair)

BERNARD PRADEL CELLARS
2100 Hoffman Lane Yountville CA 94599
Cabernet Sauvignon,'86, Napa Vly. (2)

PRESTON VINEYARDS
9282 W. Dry Creek Rd. Healdsburg CA 95448
Cabernet Sauvignon,'86, Dry Creek Vly., Estate (B-San Diego)
Cabernet Sauvignon,'87, Dry Creek Vly. $12.00 (2)
Chenin Blanc,'89, Dry Creek Vly., Estate $7.50 (3)
Sauvignon Blanc,'89, Dry Creek Vly., Cuvee De Fume $8.00 (3)
Sauvignon Blanc,'89, Dry Creek Vly., Estate Reserve $10.00 (4)
Zinfandel,'87, Dry Creek Vly. $10.00 (2)

Q

QUAFF WINERY
3354 River Rd. Windsor CA 95492
Gewurztraminer,'89, Sonoma Co. $6.25 (4)

QUAIL RIDGE WINERY
1055 Atlas Peak Rd. Napa CA 94558
Cabernet Sauvignon,'85, Napa Vly. (B-Dallas)
Sauvignon Blanc,'88, Napa Vly. (S-Dallas)

QUIVIRA VINEYARDS
4900 W. Dry Creek Rd. Healdsburg CA 95448
Cabernet Sauvignon,'87, Dry Creek Vly. $14.50 (3)
Sauvignon Blanc,'88, Dry Creek Vly. $9.25 (3)
Sauvignon Blanc,'89, Dry Creek Vly. $9.25 (S-San Fran)
Zinfandel,'88, Dry Creek Vly. $12.00 (4)

R

RABBIT RIDGE VINEYARDS
3291 Westside Rd. Healdsburg CA 95448
Cabernet Sauvignon,'85, Sonoma Co. (B-Orange)
Cabernet Sauvignon,'86, Russian River Vly. $12.00 (3)
Cabernet Sauvignon,'87, Russian River Vly. (B-Nat'l O.S.)
Chardonnay,'88, Russian River Vly., Rabbit Ridge Ranch $14.00 (5)
Chardonnay,'88, Sonoma Co. (3)
Merlot,'87, Sonoma Co., Clairvaux Vnyd. $12.00 (5)
Zinfandel,'87, Russian River Vly., Rabbit Ridge Ranch $8.00 (4)

A. RAFANELLI WINERY
4685 West Dry Creek Road Healdsburg CA 95448
Cabernet Sauvignon,'87, Dry Creek Vly. $11.50 (5)
Zinfandel,'88, Dry Creek Vly. $9.75 (4)

RANCHO SISQUOC
Rt. 1, Box 147 Santa Maria CA 93454
Johannisberg Riesling,'89, Santa Maria Vly. (S-Orange)
Merlot,'87, Santa Maria Vly. (S-Orange)

KENT RASMUSSEN WINERY
2125 Cuttings Wharf Rd. Napa CA 94559
Chardonnay,'88, Napa Vly., Carneros (B-San Diego)

Pinot Noir,'88, Carneros $18.00 (B-State Fair)

RAVENSWOOD

21415 Broadway Sonoma CA 95476

Cabernet Sauvignon,'87, Sonoma Co.   (B-Orange)
Meritage Red,'87, Sonoma Mtns., Pickberry Vnyd.   (G-Orange)
Merlot,'87, Sonoma Co.   (B-Orange)
Zinfandel,'88, North Coast, Vintner Blend   (G-Orange)

RAYMOND VINEYARD

849 Zinfandel Lane St Helena CA 94574

Cabernet Sauvignon,'85, Napa Vly.   (B-W.Coast)
Cabernet Sauvignon,'85, Napa Vly., Reserve $24.00 (2)
Cabernet Sauvignon,'86, Napa $16.00 (B-San Fran)
Chardonnay,'87, Napa Vly.   (G-W.Coast)
Chardonnay,'88, Napa Vly.   (B-L.A.)
Sauvignon Blanc,'88, Napa Vly.   (2)

RENAISSANCE VINEYARD

P. O. Box 1000 Renaissance CA 95962

Cabernet Sauvignon,'82, Sierra Foothills, Da Vinci $9.50 (S-Farmers)
Johannisberg Riesling,'85, North Yuba, LH $25.00 (S-San Fran)
Johannisberg Riesling,'88, North Yuba $8.00 (2)
Sauvignon Blanc,'83, North Yuba, LH $20.00 (2)
Sauvignon Blanc,'87, North Yuba   (B-Dallas)

REVERE VINEYARDS

2456 Third Ave. Napa CA 94548

Chardonnay,'88, Napa, Reserve $22.00 (2)

L. W. RICHARDS WINERY

7360 Perry Creek Rd. Somerset CA 95684

Cabernet Sauvignon,'85, El Dorado $14.00 (B-State Fair)

RICHARDSON VINEYARDS

2711 Knob Hill Rd. Sonoma CA 95476

Merlot,'88, Sonoma Vly., Los Carneros, Gregory $14.00 (3)
Pinot Noir,'88, Sonoma Vly., Carneros, Sangiacomo   (2)
Zinfandel,'88, Sonoma Vly. $12.00 (3)

RIDGE VINEYARDS

17100 Monte Bello Rd. Cupertino CA 95015

Zinfandel,'87, California, Howell Mtn.   (G-Orange)
Zinfandel,'87, California, Paso Robles   (B-Orange)

RIVER RUN VINTNERS

65 Rogge Lane Watsonville CA 95076

Cabernet Sauvignon,'87, Mendocino Co.   (B-W.Coast)
Zinfandel,'88, California $8.00 (2)
Zinfandel,'88, Cienega Vly., LH   (2)

RIVERBREAK CELLARS

Address not available

Pinot Noir,'88, Santa Barbara Co.   (G-Orange)
Sauvignon Blanc,'88, Santa Barbara Co.   (G-Orange)

RIVERSIDE FARM

12707 Old Redwood Hwy. Healdsburg CA 95448

Chardonnay,'89, California   (B-Orange)

ROCHE WINERY
28700 Arnold Dr. Sonoma CA 95476
Chardonnay,'88, Carneros (B-San Diego)
Pinot Noir,'88, Carneros (2)
ROCHIOLI
6192 Westside Rd. Healdsburg CA 95448
Chardonnay,'88, Russian River Vly., Estate (B-Orange)
ROMBAUER VINEYARDS
3522 Silverado Trail St Helena CA 94574
Cabernet Sauvignon,'86, Napa Vly. (S-Nat'l O.S.)
Meritage Red,'85, Napa Vly., Le Meilleur Du Chai (G-Orange)
ROSENBLUM CELLARS
1401 Stanford Ave. Emeryville CA 94608
Cabernet Sauvignon,'87, Napa, Holbrook Mitchell (B-San Diego)
Johannisberg Riesling,'89, Russian River Vly. $7.50 (S-Farmers)
Merlot,'88, Napa Vly. (2)
Petite Sirah,'88, Napa Vly. $9.95 (2)
Pinot Noir,'88, Russian River Vly. (B-Orange)
White Zinfandel,'89, Costra Costa Co. (G-L.A.)
Zinfandel,'87, Sonoma Co., Mauritson & Cullinan (B-San Diego)
Zinfandel,'88, Napa Vly, Hendry Vnyd. $11.00 (G-State Fair)
Zinfandel,'88, Sonoma Co. $9.95 (5)
Zinfandel,'NV, California, Vintners Cuvee II $6.95 (4)
Zinfandel,'NV, California, Vintners Cuvee III (2)
ROUDON-SMITH VINEYARDS
2364 Bean Creek Rd. Santa Cruz CA 95066
Cabernet Sauvignon,'84, Sonoma (S-San Diego)
Petite Sirah,'86, San Luis Obispo (B-San Diego)
Zinfandel,'88, Sonoma Vly. (B-Orange)
ROUND HILL CELLARS
1680 Silverado Trail St Helena CA 94574
Cabernet Sauvignon,'87, Napa Vly. (3)
Cabernet Sauvignon,'88, Napa Vly. (B-Nat'l O.S.)
Cabernet Sauvignon,'NV, California, House, Lot 7 $5.49 (3)
Chardonnay,'88, California, House (B-Orange)
Chardonnay,'88, Napa Vly., Reserve $8.75 (2)
Gewurztraminer,'88, Napa Vly. (S-Nat'l O.S.)
Merlot,'86, Napa Vly. (B-Nat'l O.S.)
Merlot,'87, Napa Reserve $8.99 (3)
Sauvignon Blanc,'87, Napa Vly., House Fume (G-Orange)
Zinfandel,'87, Napa Vly. $5.50 (3)
ROYAL KEDEM
Address not available
Chardonnay,'89, Sonoma $10.50 (B-San Fran)
Chenin Blanc,'89, California $5.00 (B-San Fran)
Johannisberg Riesling,'89, California, LH $7.50 (B-San Fran)
Sauvignon Blanc,'89, California $7.50 (B-San Fran)
RUTHERFORD ESTATE CELLARS
Address not available
White Zinfandel,'89, Napa Vly. (G-Orange)

RUTHERFORD HILL WINERY
200 Rutherford Hill Rd. Rutherford CA 94573
Cabernet Sauvignon,'85, Napa Vly. (B-Dallas)
Chardonnay,'86, Napa Vly., Reserve (G-Orange)
Chardonnay,'87, Napa Vly., Rutherford Knoll (B-Dallas)

RUTHERFORD RANCH
1680 Silverado Trail St Helena CA 94574
Cabernet Sauvignon,'85, Rutherford Ranch $10.50 (2)
Zinfandel,'87, Napa Vly. (B-Dallas)

RUTHERFORD VINTNERS
1673 St. Helena Hwy. So. Rutherford CA 94573
Cabernet Sauvignon,'78, Napa Vly. $22.50 (2)
Cabernet Sauvignon,'79, Napa Vly. $16.00 (B-State Fair)
Cabernet Sauvignon,'81, Napa, Reserve $16.50 (B-San Fran)
Cabernet Sauvignon,'84, Napa $12.50 (S-San Fran)
Chardonnay,'87, Napa Vly. (B-San Diego)
Johannisberg Riesling,'86, Napa $8.00 (S-San Fran)
Sauvignon Blanc,'87, Napa Vly. $8.00 (2)

SADDLEBACK CELLARS
7802 Money Rd. Oakville CA 94562
Cabernet Sauvignon,'86, Napa Vly, Estate (B-Orange)

SAINTSBURY WINERY
1500 Los Carneros Ave. Napa CA 94558
Chardonnay,'88, Carneros $14.00 (2)
Chardonnay,'88, Carneros, Reserve $20.00 (2)
Pinot Noir,'88, Carneros $15.00 (2)

SANFORD WINERY
7250 Santa Rosa Rd. Buellton CA 93427
Chardonnay,'88, Santa Barbara Co. (B-Dallas)
Pinot Noir,'86, Santa Barbara Co., Barrel Select (S-Orange)
Pinot Noir,'87, Santa Barbara Co. $14.50 (2)
Sauvignon Blanc,'88, Santa Barbara Co. (B-Dallas)

SANTA BARBARA WINERY
202 Anacapa St. Santa Barbara CA 93101
Cabernet Sauvignon,'87, Santa Ynez Vly., Reserve (2)
Chardonnay,'88, Santa Ynez Vly. (3)
Chardonnay,'88, Santa Ynez Vly., Reserve $18.00 (4)
Chenin Blanc,'88, Santa Ynez Vly., Barrel Ferm. (2)
Johannisberg Riesling,'88, (B-L.A.)
Johannisberg Riesling,'88, Santa Ynez Vly., Paradis Dry $7.50 (2)
Pinot Noir,'88, Santa Ynez Vly. (2)
Pinot Noir,'88, Santa Ynez Vly., Reserve $20.00 (2)
Sauvignon Blanc,'88, Santa Ynez Vly. $9.00 (2)
Sauvignon Blanc,'88, Santa Ynez Vly., Reserve $12.00 (2)
White Zinfandel,'89, Central Coast $6.75 (B-San Fran)
Zinfandel,'89, Santa Ynez Vly., Boujour $7.50 (2)

SANTA YNEZ WINERY
P. O. Box 558 Santa Ynez CA 93460
Johannisberg Riesling,'89, Santa Ynez Vly., Reserve (B-L.A.)
Johannisberg Riesling,'89, Santa Ynez Vly. (G-Orange)

Meritage Red,'87, Santa Barbara Co. (B-Orange)

SANTINO WINES
Rt. 2, Box 21-A Plymouth CA 95669
White Zinfandel,'89, White Harvest (B-L.A.)
Zinfandel,'85, Amador Co., Aged Release (S-Orange)
Zinfandel,'85, Fiddletown (B-Dallas)
Zinfandel,'86, Shenandoah Vly., Grandpere Vnyd. $12.00 (3)
Zinfandel,'87, Shenandoah Vly., Grandpere Vnyd. $12.00 (2)

V. SATTUI WINERY
White Lane & Hwy. 29 St Helena CA 94574
Cabernet Sauvignon,'84, Napa, Preston, Reserve (B-Nat'l O.S.)
Cabernet Sauvignon,'86, Napa Vly. $12.95 (5)
Cabernet Sauvignon,'87, Napa Vly., Preston Vnyd. $16.95 (3)
Chardonnay,'88, Napa Vly. $13.95 (B-Farmers)
Johannisberg Riesling,'89, Napa Vly., Dry $8.50 (3)
Johannisberg Riesling,'89, Napa Vly., Off Dry $8.50 (3)
Sauvignon Blanc,'88, Napa Vly., Suzanne's Vnyd., Lot 2 (G-Dallas)
Sauvignon Blanc,'89, Napa Vly., Suzanne's Vnyd., Estate $8.95 (2)
White Zinfandel,'89, California $6.95 (5)
Zinfandel,'84, Napa Vly., Howell Mtn., Reserve (2)
Zinfandel,'86, Napa Vly, Howell Mtn. $10.95 (2)
Zinfandel,'87, Napa Vly., Howell Mtn. $10.95 (B-Farmers)
Zinfandel,'87, Napa Vly., Suzanne's Vnyd. $10.95 (3)

SAUCELITO CANYON VINEYARDS
1600 Saucelito Creek Rd. Arroyo Grande CA 93420
Zinfandel,'87, San Luis Obispo Co. (2)
Zinfandel,'88, San Luis Obispo Co. $11.00 (S-State Fair)

SAUSAL WINERY
7370 Highway 128 Healdsburg CA 95448
Zinfandel,'87, Alexander Vly. $7.50 (B-Farmers)
Zinfandel,'88, Alexander Vly. (S-W.Coast)

SCHARFFENBERGER
307 Talmadge Rd. Ukiah CA 95482
Sparkling Wine,'NV, Mendocino Co., Brut Rose (B-Orange)

SCHRAMSBERG
Schramsberg Rd. Calistoga CA 94515
Sparkling Wine,'86, Napa Vly., Blanc De Blanc (B-Orange)

SCHUG CELLARS
6204 St. Helena Hwy. Yountville CA 94599
Chardonnay,'87, Carneros, Beckstoffer Vnyd. $14.75 (3)

SEA RIDGE WINERY
P. O. Box 433 Cazadero CA 95421
Pinot Noir,'88, Sonoma Coast $11.75 (2)

SEBASTIANI VINEYARDS
389 Fourth St. E. Sonoma CA 95476
Cabernet Sauvignon,'85, Sonoma Co., Reserve $11.00 (4)
Cabernet Sauvignon,'86, Sonoma Co. (B-Orange)
Cabernet Sauvignon,'87, Sonoma Co. $8.00 (2)
Cabernet Sauvignon,'88, California (S-W.Coast)
Cabernet Sauvignon,'NV, California, Country $8.00 (B-Farmers)
Chardonnay,'88, Sonoma Co., Reserve $10.00 (2)
Chardonnay,'NV, California, Country $8.00 (B-Farmers)

Johannisberg Riesling,'88, California, Country $8.00 (B-Farmers)
Meritage Red,'87, Sonoma, Wildwood Red $12.99 (B-State Fair)
Merlot,'87, Sonoma Co. $7.50 (B-Farmers)
Merlot,'88, Sonoma Co. $7.00 (2)
Sparkling Wine,'85, Richard Cuneo Cuvee $15.00 (5)
Sparkling Wine,'NV, Sonoma Co. Brut, Five Star $10.00 (B-State Fair)
Sparkling Wine,'NV, Sonoma Co., Blanc De Noir (2)
White Zinfandel,'89, Sonoma Co., Dry $4.99 (B-Farmers)
Zinfandel,'87, Sonoma Co. $6.00 (6)

SEGHESIO WINERY
14730 Grove St. Healdsburg CA 95448
Cabernet Sauvignon,'86, Northern Sonoma Co. (2)
Chardonnay,'88, Sonoma Co., Reserve $12.00 (2)
Chenin Blanc,'88, Northern Sonoma, Dry (B-Orange)
Pinot Noir,'87, Russian River Vly. (2)
Pinot Noir,'87, Russian River, Reserve $12.00 (2)
Zinfandel,'87, Northern Sonoma $6.00 (3)

SELLARDS WINERY
6400 Sequoia Circle Sebastopol CA 95472
Cabernet Sauvignon,'86, Alex. Vly., Warnecke Vnyds. $14.00
Chardonnay,'88, Russian River Vly., Graton Hills Vnyd. (2)

SEQUOIA GROVE VINEYARDS
8338 St. Helena Hwy. Napa CA 94558
Cabernet Sauvignon,'86, Napa $16.00 (2)
Cabernet Sauvignon,'86, Napa, Estate $22.00 (B-San Fran)
Cabernet Sauvignon,'87, Napa Co. $16.00 (2)
Cabernet Sauvignon,'87, Napa Vly., Estate $22.00 (5)
Chardonnay,'88, Napa Vly., Carneros $14.00 (B-San Fran)
Chardonnay,'88, Napa Vly., Estate (3)
Gewurztraminer,'89, Allen Family Vnyd. (G-L.A.)

SHADOW CREEK CELLARS
California Drive Yountville CA 94599
Sparkling Wine,'83, California, Brut, Reserve $16.00 (5)
Sparkling Wine,'NV, California, Blanc De Noirs $10.99 (2)
Sparkling Wine,'NV, California, Brut $10.99 (4)

SHAFER VINEYARDS
6154 Silverado Trail Napa CA 94558
Cabernet Sauvignon,'85, Stags Leap, Hillside Select (S-Dallas)
Cabernet Sauvignon,'87, Napa Vly., Stag's Leap Dist. $17.00 (3)
Chardonnay,'88, Napa $13.50 (2)
Merlot,'87, Napa Vly. (B-Dallas)
Merlot,'88, Napa $16.50 (2)

CHARLES F. SHAW WINERY
1010 Big Tree Road St Helena CA 94558
Chardonnay,'88, Napa Vly. $10.50 (2)
Pinot Noir,'87, Napa Vly., Carneros $14.50 (4)
Sauvignon Blanc,'88, Napa Vly. (2)
Sauvignon Blanc,'89, Napa Vly. $9.50 (4)

SHENANDOAH VINEYARDS
12300 Steiner Rd. Plymouth CA 95669
Johannisberg Riesling,'88, Shenandoah Vly. (B-Nat'l O.S.)
Sauvignon Blanc,'89, Amador $7.75 (2)
White Zinfandel,'89, Amador Co. (B-Nat'l O.S.)

Zinfandel,'88, Amador Co., Reserve $7.75 (B-State Fair)

SIERRA VISTA
4560 Cabernet Way Placerville CA 95667
Chardonnay,'87, El Dorado, Estate (B-Orange)

SIGNORELLO VINEYARDS
4500 Silverado Trail Napa CA 94558
Chardonnay,'88, Napa Vly., Estate $14.50 (S-Farmers)

SILVER CANYON
Address not available
Chardonnay,'89, (B-L.A.)

SILVERADO HILL CELLARS
P. O. Box 2640 Napa CA 94558
Chardonnay,'88, Napa Vly. (B-Orange)
Chardonnay,'88, Napa, Private Cellar $13.00 (B-San Fran)

SILVERADO VINEYARDS
6121 Silverado Trail Napa CA 94558
Cabernet Sauvignon,'87, Napa Vly. (B-Orange)
Sauvignon Blanc,'89, Napa Vly. $9.00 (B-San Fran)

SIMI WINERY
16275 Healdsburg Ave. Healdsburg CA 95448
Cabernet Sauvignon,'82, Sonoma/Napa, Reserve (B-Dallas)
Cabernet Sauvignon,'85, Sonoma Co. (B-Dallas)
Cabernet Sauvignon,'86, Alexander Vly. $15.00 (B-State Fair)
Chardonnay,'88, Sonoma/Mendocino/Napa $15.75 (2)
Chenin Blanc,'88, Mendocino Co. $6.00 (2)
Chenin Blanc,'89, Mendocino Co. $6.00 (5)
Sauvignon Blanc,'87, Sonoma Co. (S-Dallas)
Sauvignon Blanc,'88, Sonoma Co. $8.50 (4)

ROBERT SINSKEY VINEYARDS
6320 Silverado Trail Napa CA 94558
Chardonnay,'87, Napa Vly., Carneros (2)
Chardonnay,'88, Napa Vly., Carneros, Estate $16.00 (B-San Fran)
Merlot,'87, Napa Vly. $18.00 (G-State Fair)
Pinot Noir,'87, Napa Vly., Carneros (S-Dallas)
Pinot Noir,'88, Napa Vly., Carneros, Estate $18.00 (2)

SMITH & HOOK WINERY
37700 Foothill Rd. Soledad CA 93960
Cabernet Sauvignon,'85, Monterey Co. (2)
Cabernet Sauvignon,'86, Monterey Co. $15.00 (B-State Fair)
Merlot,'87, Monterey, Estate $15.00 (B-San Fran)

SOLANO WINERY
Address not available
Gewurztraminer,'NV, North Coast $3.00 (S-State Fair)

SOLARI ESTATE
1310 Bennett Lane Calistoga CA 94515
Cabernet Sauvignon,'86, Napa, Larkmead Vnyds. $10.50 (S-State
Merlot,'87, Napa Vly., Dutch Henry Vnyds., Estate $11.00 (2)

SONOMA CREEK WINERY
23355 Millerick Road Sonoma CA 95476
Chardonnay,'88, Carneros $12.00 (2)

SONOMA CUTRER

4401 Slusser Rd. Windsor CA 95492

Chardonnay,'88, Russian River Ranches, Estate (B-Orange)

SONORA WINERY

P. O. Box 242 Sonora CA 95370

Zinfandel,'88, Dry Creek Vly. (B-Orange)

SOQUEL WINERY

3875 Trout Gulch Rd. Aptos CA 95003

Chardonnay,'88, Trout Gulch Vnyd. (S-Nat'l O.S.)

SPRING MOUNTAIN VINEYARDS

2805 Spring Mtn. Rd. St Helena CA 94574

Cabernet Sauvignon,'86, Napa Vly. (G-Orange)
Chardonnay,'87, Napa Vly. (S-Dallas)
Chardonnay,'88, Napa Vly. $13.50 (S-State Fair)

ST. ANDREWS WINERY

2921 Silverado Trail Napa CA 94558

Chardonnay,'87, Napa Vly., Estate $13.25 (2)
Chardonnay,'88, Napa Vly. $10.00 (3)
Chardonnay,'88, Napa Vly., Estate $13.25 (B-San Fran)
Sauvignon Blanc,'87, Napa Vly. $7.50 (2)

ST. CLEMENT VINEYARDS

2867 St. Helena Hwy. N. St Helena CA 94574

Cabernet Sauvignon,'82, Napa Vly. (S-L.A.)
Cabernet Sauvignon,'84, Napa Vly. (B-L.A.)
Cabernet Sauvignon,'85, Napa Vly. $17.00 (2)
Chardonnay,'87, Napa Vly., Carneros, Abbotts Vnyd. (B-Orange)
Chardonnay,'88, Napa Vly., Carneros, Abbotts Vnyd. (2)
Merlot,'86, Napa Vly. $15.00 (5)
Sauvignon Blanc,'89, Napa Vly. $9.75 (4)

ST. FRANCIS WINERY

8450 Sonoma Hwy. Kenwood CA 95452

Cabernet Sauvignon,'86, Sonoma Co. (B-San Diego)
Cabernet Sauvignon,'87, Sonoma Vly. $20.00 (4)
Chardonnay,'88, California $10.00 (3)
Chardonnay,'88, Sonoma Vly., Estate $15.00 (2)
Gewurztraminer,'89, Sonoma Co. $7.50 (5)
Johannisberg Riesling,'88, Sonoma Vly., Estate (B-L.A.)
Merlot,'86, Sonoma Vly. (S-Dallas)
Merlot,'87, Sonoma Vly., Estate $18.00 (2)

ST. SUPERY VINEYARDS

8440 St. Helena Hwy. Rutherford CA 94573

Cabernet Sauvignon,'87, Napa Vly., Dollarhide Ranch (4)
Chardonnay,'88, Napa Vly. $11.00 (2)
Sauvignon Blanc,'88, Napa Vly., Dollarhide Ranch $7.50 (4)

STAG'S LEAP WINE CELLARS

5766 Silverado Trail Napa CA 94558

Chardonnay,'88, Napa Vly. $18.00 (2)

LELAND STANFORD WINERY

P. O. Box 3398 Mission San Jose CA 94538

Sparkling Wine,'NV, California, Hilton Brut $9.00 (B-Farmers)
Sparkling Wine,'NV, California, Hilton Extra Dry (B-L.A.)

STELZNER VINEYARDS
5998 Silverado Trail Napa CA 94588
Cabernet Sauvignon,'86, Napa Vly., Estate $16.00 (3)

ROBERT STEMMLER WINERY
3805 Lambert Bridge Rd. Healdsburg CA 95448
Pinot Noir,'86, Sonoma Co. (B-Dallas)

STERLING VINEYARDS
1111 Dunaweal Lane Calistoga CA 94515
Cabernet Sauvignon,'86, Napa, Diamond Mt. Ranch $16.00 (2)
Chardonnay,'88, Napa Vly. $14.50 (2)
Meritage Red,'86, Napa Vly., Reserve $45.00 (3)
Meritage Red,'86, Napa Vly., Three Palms Red (3)
Merlot,'87, Napa Vly., Estate (B-Orange)
Pinot Noir,'87, Napa Vly., Carneros, Winery Lake $16.00 (4)
Sauvignon Blanc,'88, Napa Vly (B-W.Coast)

STEVENOT WINERY
2690 San Domingo Rd. Murphys CA 95247
Cabernet Sauvignon,'85, Calaveras Co., Grand Reserve (2)
Chardonnay,'87, Calaveras Co., Grand Reserve (G-Dallas)
Chardonnay,'88, Calaveras Co., Grand Reserve $10.00 (4)
Chenin Blanc,'89, Sierra Foothills (S-W.Coast)
Sauvignon Blanc,'89, Amador Co. (B-W.Coast)
Zinfandel,'87, Calaveras Co., Grand Reserve $10.00 (S-San Fran)

STONE CREEK
543 Forbes Blvd. So San Francisco CA 94080
Cabernet Sauvignon,'83, Mendocino Co. (B-San Diego)
Cabernet Sauvignon,'86, Napa, Ltd. Bottling $9.00 (B-San Fran)
Chardonnay,'87, Napa Vly., Special Selection (G-Orange)
Chardonnay,'88, Alexander Vly. $9.00 (2)
Chardonnay,'NV, American (B-San Diego)
Sauvignon Blanc,'87, Napa Vly., Special Sel. Fume (2)

STONEGATE WINERY
1183 Dunaweal Lane Calistoga CA 94515
Chardonnay,'87, Napa Vly. (B-San Diego)
Merlot,'86, Napa, Estate $15.00 (2)

STONY RIDGE WINERY
818 Main Street Pleasanton CA 94566
Cabernet Sauvignon,'NV, California $6.00 (B-Farmers)
Chardonnay,'87, Napa Vly., Ltd. Release (B-San Diego)
Chardonnay,'89, California $5.50 (G-State Fair)
Meritage Red,'84, North Coast, Ltd. Release (S-Orange)
White Zinfandel,'89, California (3)

STORRS WINERY
303 Potrero St. #35 Santa Cruz CA 95060
Johannisberg Riesling,'89, Monterey $7.00 (S-San Fran)
Johannisberg Riesling,'89, Santa Cruz Mtns. $9.00 (4)

STORYBOOK MT. VINEYARDS
3835 Hwy. 128 Calistoga CA 94515
Zinfandel,'86, Napa Vly. $12.00 (3)
Zinfandel,'86, Napa Vly., Estate (B-San Diego)
Zinfandel,'86, Sonoma Co. (B-Dallas)
Zinfandel,'87, Napa Vly, Reserve $17.50 (B-San Fran)

Zinfandel,'87, Napa Vly. $11.50 (4)

STRATFORD WINERY
1472 Railroad Ave. St Helena CA 94574
Cabernet Sauvignon,'87, Napa Vly. (S-San Diego)
Chardonnay,'88, California (B-Orange)
Merlot,'88, California $11.00 (B-San Fran)
Sauvignon Blanc,'88, California $8.00 (G-Farmers)

STRAUS VINEYARDS
P. O. Box 10 St Helena CA 94574
Merlot,'87, Napa Vly. (B-Dallas)
Merlot,'88, Napa Vly. (2)

STREBLOW VINEYARDS
P. O. Box 233 St Helena CA 94574
Cabernet Sauvignon,'87, Napa Vly., Estate $16.00 (S-State Fair)
Chardonnay,'88, California $15.00 (B-San Fran)

RODNEY STRONG VINEYARDS
11455 Old Redwood Hwy. Windsor CA 95492
Cabernet Sauvignon,'84, Alexander's Crown (2)
Cabernet Sauvignon,'85, Alexander's Crown Vnyd. $16.00 (6)
Cabernet Sauvignon,'86, Sonoma Co. (B-Dallas)
Cabernet Sauvignon,'87, Sonoma Co. $9.00 (5)
Chardonnay,'86, Chalk Hill (B-Dallas)
Chardonnay,'87, Sonoma Co., Chalk Hill Vnyd. $12.00 (4)
Chardonnay,'88, Chalk Hill $12.00 (3)
Chardonnay,'89, Sonoma Co. (B-San Diego)
Gewurztraminer,'89, Sonoma Co. (B-W.Coast)
Johannisberg Riesling,'86, Le Baron Vnyd., LH $9.00 (5)
Merlot,'86, Russian River Vly., Vintner Grown $10.00 (B-San Fran)
Pinot Noir,'85, River East Vnyd., Estate $10.00 (5)
Sauvignon Blanc,'87, Charlotte's Home Vnyd. Fume $9.00 (3)
Zinfandel,'86, Sonoma Co. (B-Dallas)

SUMMIT LAKE VINEYARDS
2000 Summit Lake Dr. Angwin CA 94508
Zinfandel,'85, Napa Vly., Howell Mtn. (S-Orange)

SUNNY ST. HELENA WINERY
1000 Main St. St Helena CA 94574
Cabernet Sauvignon,'86, Napa Vly. $10.85 (S-State Fair)

SUNRISE WINERY
13100 Montebello Rd. Cupertino CA 95015
Cabernet Sauvignon,'86, Santa Cruz, Arata Vnyd. $13.00 (B-State
Chardonnay,'88, Santa Clara, San Ysidro $14.00 (B-State Fair)
Johannisberg Riesling,'88, Santa Clara Co. (B-L.A.)

SUTTER HOME WINERY
277 St. Helena Hwy So. St Helena CA 94574
Cabernet Sauvignon,'88, California $5.00 (B-San Fran)
Sauvignon Blanc,'88, California (G-Orange)
White Zinfandel,'89, California (B-Orange)

SWANSON WINERY
1271 Manley Lane Rutherford CA 94573
Cabernet Sauvignon,'87, Napa Vly. $18.50 (2)
Chardonnay,'88, Napa Vly. $14.95 (4)
Chardonnay,'88, Napa Vly., Reserve $18.50 (3)

Merlot,'88, Napa Vly $15.00 (2)
Zinfandel,'88, Napa Vly., Estate $15.00 (B-State Fair)

SYCAMORE CREEK WINERY

12775 Uvas Rd. Morgan Hill CA 95037

Johannisberg Riesling,'87, Romeo & Juliet $20.00 (S-State Fair)
Johannisberg Riesling,'89, Bien Nacido Vnyd. $8.00 (S-State Fair)

T

TAFT STREET WINERY

6450 First St. Forestville CA 95436
Chardonnay,'88, Russian River Vly. $11.50 (4)
Chardonnay,'89, Sonoma Co. $8.50 (6)
Sauvignon Blanc,'88, Napa $7.00 (2)

TAYLOR CALIFORNIA CELLARS

800 S. Alta Street Gonzales CA 93926

Chardonnay,'89, California, Classic (B-Orange)
Chenin Blanc,'NV, California (B-Dallas)

TEADERIPPLE

Address not available

Sauvignon Blanc,'89, Napa Vly., Teaderman (S-Orange)

TERRA

Address not available

Chardonnay,'87, Napa Vly. (S-Orange)

TERRA ROSA

Address not available

Meritage Red,'87, Napa Vly. (G-Orange)

TIJSSELING VINEYARDS

2150 Mc Nab Ranch Rd. Ukiah CA 95482
Sparkling Wine,'85, Mendocino Co. (B-W.Coast)
Sparkling Wine,'86, Mendocino Co. (S-W.Coast)
Sparkling Wine,'87, Mendocino Co., Brut (G-L.A.)

TOPOLOS AT RUSSIAN RIVER

5700 Gravenstein Hwy N. Forestville CA 95436
Zinfandel,'87, Sonoma Co., Rossi Ranch (2)
Zinfandel,'88, Sonoma Co. (B-Orange)

TOTT'S CHAMPAGNE CELLARS

600 Yosemite Blvd. Modesto CA 95353
Sparkling Wine,'NV, California, Brut $7.50 (5)
Sparkling Wine,'NV, Extra Dry $7.50 (3)

TRADER JOE'S

538 Mission Street So Pasadena CA 91030
Chardonnay,'89, Sonoma Co. (B-Orange)
Johannisberg Riesling,'89, Monterey Co. (G-Orange)
Sparkling Wine,'NV, Mendocino Co., Brut (G-Orange)

TREFETHEN VINEYARDS

1160 Oak Knoll Ave. Napa CA 94558
Cabernet Sauvignon,'86, Napa Vly. (S-Dallas)
Chardonnay,'87, Napa, Estate $16.75 (5)
Johannisberg Riesling,'89, Napa Vly., White, Estate $8.75 (6)
Pinot Noir,'86, Napa Vly. $12.75 (B-Farmers)

TRENTADUE WINERY
19170 Redwood Hwy. Geyserville CA 95441

Cabernet Sauvignon,'86, Sonoma Co., Estate $11.00 (S-State Fair)
Merlot,'86, Sonoma Co. (B-L.A.)

M. TRIBAUT
1005 Market St. #305 San Francisco CA 94103

Sparkling Wine,'85, Monterey Co., Rose (2)
Sparkling Wine,'NV, Monterey Co., Brut (S-Orange)
Sparkling Wine,'NV, Monterey, Blanc De Noirs (2)

TROUT GULCH VINEYARDS
Address not available

Chardonnay,'88, Santa Cruz Mtns. (S-Orange)
Pinot Noir,'88, Santa Cruz Mtns. (B-Orange)

TULOCAY WINERY
1426 Coombsville Napa CA 94558

Cabernet Sauvignon,'87, Napa Vly. (2)
Chardonnay,'88, Napa Vly, De Celles Vnyd. (B-Orange)

V

M. G. VALLEJO WINERY
1883 London Ranch Rd. Glen Ellen CA 95442

Cabernet Sauvignon,'87, California $5.75 (2)
Chardonnay,'88, California $5.75 (B-Farmers)
Chardonnay,'89, California (2)
Sauvignon Blanc,'89, California $5.00 (B-San Fran)
White Zinfandel,'89, California $4.75 (7)
Zinfandel,'83, California, Bi-Centennial (B-Nat'l O.S.)

VALLEY OF THE MOON WINERY
777 Madrona Rd. Glen Ellen CA 95442

Cabernet Sauvignon,'87, Sonoma Vly., Reserve $12.00 (5)
Chardonnay,'89, (G-L.A.)
White Zinfandel,'89, California $5.50 (2)
Zinfandel,'84, Sonoma Vly. (B-Nat'l O.S.)
Zinfandel,'84, Sonoma Vly., Estate Reserve $9.25 (S-Farmers)

VAN DER KAMP CHAMPAGNE
307 Warm Springs Road Kenwood CA 95452

Sparkling Wine,'83, Sonoma Vly., Brut Reserve (B-Orange)
Sparkling Wine,'84, Sonoma Vly. (B-W.Coast)
Sparkling Wine,'87, Sonoma, Midnight Cuvee (4)

VENDANGE
389 4th St. E. Sonoma CA 95476

Cabernet Sauvignon,'88, California (B-Orange)
Merlot,'89, California (2)
White Zinfandel,'89, California $4.49 (3)
Zinfandel,'87, California (B-Orange)

VENTANA VINEYARDS
2999 Monterey Salinas Hwy. Monterey CA 93940

Chardonnay,'88, Monterey, Crystal $16.00 (2)
Chardonnay,'89, Monterey, Gold Stripe $10.00 (S-San Fran)
Johannisberg Riesling,'87, Monterey, LH $10.00 (2)
Johannisberg Riesling,'88, Monterey $6.50 (4)
Johannisberg Riesling,'89, Monterey, Dry $6.50 (3)

Sauvignon Blanc,'87, Monterey, Ventana Vnyd. (S-Orange)
Sauvignon Blanc,'88, Monterey $8.00 (3)
Sauvignon Blanc,'89, Monterey $8.00 (3)

VIANSA WINERY
461 7th St. West Sonoma CA 95476
Sauvignon Blanc,'87, Sonoma / Napa (B-Dallas)

VICHON WINERY
1595 Oakville Grade Oakville CA 94562
Cabernet Sauvignon,'87, Napa Vly., Stags Leap Dist. $23.00 (2)
Chardonnay,'88, Napa Vly. $16.00 (5)
Meritage White,'88, Napa Vly. $9.50 (2)
Merlot,'87, Napa Vly. $16.00 (3)
Merlot,'88, Napa Vly. $16.00 (4)

VILLA HELENA
1455 Inglewood Ave. St Helena CA 94574
Chardonnay,'88, Napa Vly., McGrath Vnyd., Estate (S-Orange)

VILLA MT. EDEN WINERY
620 Oakville Cross Rd. Oakville CA 94562
Cabernet Sauvignon,'85, Napa Vly., Estate $12.00 (3)
Chenin Blanc,'88, Napa Vly. $5.99 (4)
Sauvignon Blanc,'89, Napa Vly., LH (2)
Zinfandel,'87, Napa Vly. (S-Dallas)
Zinfandel,'88, Napa Vly. (2)

VILLA ZAPU
P. O. Box 975 St Helena CA 94574
Chardonnay,'88, Napa Vly. $15.00 (3)

VINA VISTA VINEYARDS
14401 Chianti Rd. Geyserville CA 95441
Cabernet Sauvignon,'85, Alexander Vly., Reserve (3)
Cabernet Sauvignon,'86, Alexander Vly. (G-W.Coast)
Chardonnay,'87, Alexander Vly., Wasson Ranch (B-Dallas)

VINEYARD HILL
Address not available
Cabernet Sauvignon,'87, Mendocino Co. (S-L.A.)
Chenin Blanc,'89, Mendocino Co. (S-L.A.)

W

WARNER WEST VINEYARDS
P. O. Box 558 Solvang CA 93463
Chardonnay,'84, Santa Barbara Co., Reserve (S-Nat'l O.S.)

WEIBEL VINEYARDS
1250 Stanford Ave. Mission San Jose CA 94538
Cabernet Sauvignon,'87, Mendocino Co. (2)
Chardonnay,'88, Mendocino Co. (2)
Chardonnay,'89, Mendocino Co. (S-L.A.)
Chenin Blanc,'89, Mendocino Co., Dry (2)
Gewurztraminer,'89, Mendocino Co. $5.00 (4)
Pinot Noir,'88, Mendocino Co. $5.49 (2)
Sauvignon Blanc,'89, Mendocino Co. (B-L.A.)
Sparkling Wine,'NV, California, Sparkling Muscat $5.99 (2)

WEINSTOCK CELLARS
P. O. Box 740 Geyserville CA 95441
Chardonnay,'89, Sonoma Co. (B-W.Coast)
White Zinfandel,'89, Sonoma Co. (G-Orange)

WENTE BROS.
5565 Tesla Road Livermore CA 94550
Cabernet Sauvignon,'86, Chas. Wetmore Vnyd. Reserve $18.00
Cabernet Sauvignon,'87, Napa Vly. $8.00 (5)
Chardonnay,'88, Central Coast (S-W.Coast)
Chardonnay,'88, Central Coast, Estate Reserve $12.00 (2)
Chardonnay,'89, Central Coast $8.00 (2)
Chenin Blanc,'89, Central Coast, Le Blanc De Blanc (B-L.A.)
Gewurztraminer,'88, Arroyo Seco Vnyd., Estate Reserve (S-Dallas)
Johannisberg Riesling,'87, Arroyo Seco, Reserve $10.00 (4)
Johannisberg Riesling,'88, Arroyo Seco (B-Orange)
Sauvignon Blanc,'88, Livermore Vly., Estate Reserve $6.50 (2)
Sauvignon Blanc,'88, Livermore Vly., Fume $6.50 (S-Farmers)
Sparkling Wine,'85, Arroyo Seco, Brut (3)
Zinfandel,'86, Livermore Vly., Raboli Vnyd., Estate Reserve $8.00 (4)

WESTWOOD WINERY
Address not available
Pinot Noir,'87, Napa Vly., Haynes Vnyd., Reserve $15.00 (2)

WILLIAM WHEELER WINERY
130 Plaza Street Healdsburg CA 95448
Cabernet Sauvignon,'85, Dry Creek Vly. $15.00 (S-San Fran)
Cabernet Sauvignon,'85, Norse Vnyd., Reserve (B-San Diego)
Cabernet Sauvignon,'86, Dry Creek Vly $12.00 (B-State Fair)
Chardonnay,'88, Sonoma $12.00 (2)
Sauvignon Blanc,'88, Dry Creek Vly. $8.00 (5)
White Zinfandel,'89, Sonoma Co., Young Vines $6.50 (2)

WHITE OAK VINEYARDS
208 Haydon St. Healdsburg CA 95448
Chardonnay,'88, Sonoma Co. $12.00 (5)
Chardonnay,'88, Sonoma Co., Reserve $20.00 (7)
Chenin Blanc,'89, Alexander Vly. $6.75 (6)
Sauvignon Blanc,'89, Sonoma Co. (2)
Zinfandel,'88, Dry Creek Vly., Saunders Vnyd. $10.00 (B-State Fair)

WHITEHALL LANE WINERY
1563 St. Helena Hwy. St Helena CA 94574
Cabernet Sauvignon,'86, Napa Vly. $16.00 (4)
Cabernet Sauvignon,'87, Napa $16.00 (4)
Cabernet Sauvignon,'NV, California, Le Petite (2)
Chenin Blanc,'89, Napa Vly. (3)
Johannisberg Riesling,'89, Napa Vly., LH (S-San Diego)
Pinot Noir,'88, (S-L.A.)

WHITFORD CELLARS
4047 E. Third Ave. Napa CA 94558
Chardonnay,'88, Napa Vly. $13.00 (2)

WILD HORSE WINERY
P. O. Box 638 Templeton CA 93465
Cabernet Sauvignon,'86, Central Coast $12.00 (4)
Cabernet Sauvignon,'87, Paso Robles $12.00 (4)

Chardonnay,'88, San Luis Obispo Co. $13.00 (2)
Merlot,'88, Central Coast $13.00 (5)
Pinot Noir,'88, Santa Barbara Co. $13.00 (7)

J WILE & SONS

401 So. St. Helena Hwy. St Helena CA 94574

Cabernet Sauvignon,'87, Napa Vly. (2)
Chardonnay,'88, Napa Vly. (S-Nat'l O.S.)
Chardonnay,'88, Napa Vly. (B-Nat'l O.S.)
Chardonnay,'88, Napa Vly., Reserve (B-Dallas)
Merlot,'87, Napa Vly., Reserve (B-Dallas)

WINDMERE WINES

P. O. Box 1287 Healdsburg CA 95448

Chardonnay,'87, Edna Vly. (B-Dallas)

WINDSOR VINEYARDS

11455 Old Redwood Hwy. Healdsburg CA 95448

Cabernet Sauvignon,'84, Mendocino Co. $9.00 (4)
Cabernet Sauvignon,'85, Mendocino Co., Haehl Ranch $9.00 (2)
Cabernet Sauvignon,'85, R. B. Sayre Signature Series (G-Nat'l O.S.)
Cabernet Sauvignon,'85, Russian River Vly., Reserve $12.00 (4)
Cabernet Sauvignon,'86, Russian River Vly., Reserve $12.00 (3)
Cabernet Sauvignon,'87, Sonoma Co. (S-Orange)
Chardonnay,'86, Russian River Vly., Reserve (G-Nat'l O.S.)
Chardonnay,'87, Russian River Vly., Preston Ranch (S-Nat'l O.S.)
Chardonnay,'87, Russian River Vly., River Estates $11.00 (5)
Chardonnay,'87, Russian River Vly., Winemasters Selection (3)
Chardonnay,'88, Alexander Vly., Murphy Ranch $10.00 (4)
Chardonnay,'88, Russian River Vly., Preston Ranch $12.00 (4)
Chardonnay,'88, Sonoma Co. $8.50 (2)
Chardonnay,'88, Sonoma Co., Signature Series $13.33 (S-Farmers)
Chenin Blanc,'89, Alexander Vly. $6.00 (4)
Gewurztraminer,'87, Alexander Vly., LH $12.00 (4)
Johannisberg Riesling,'88, Sonoma Co., LH $12.00 (5)
Merlot,'85, Russian River Vly., River West Vnyd. (B-Orange)
Merlot,'86, Russian River Vly. $10.00 (5)
Petite Sirah,'86, California $7.00 (7)
Pinot Noir,'86, Los Carneros $10.00 (2)
Pinot Noir,'87, Los Carneros (B-L.A.)
Sauvignon Blanc,'88, Alexander Vly., SLH $15.00 (2)
Sparkling Wine,'86, Sonoma Co. $12.50 (4)
Sparkling Wine,'86, Sonoma, Blanc De Blanc $15.00 (3)
Sparkling Wine,'87, Sonoma Co., Blanc De Noir $13.33 (5)
Sparkling Wine,'87, Sonoma Co., Brut Rose $12.00 (4)
Sparkling Wine,'NV, R. B. Sayre Select (S-Nat'l O.S.)
White Zinfandel,'89, Sonoma Co. (S-Nat'l O.S.)
Zinfandel,'83, Russian River Vly., Reserve (S-Nat'l O.S.)
Zinfandel,'83, Russian River Vly., Reserve, LH $10.00 (2)
Zinfandel,'85, Russian River Vly., Winemasters Selection (2)

WOODSIDE VINEYARDS

340 Kings Mtn. Road Woodside CA 94062

Cabernet Sauvignon,'87, Santa Cruz Mtns. Estate $15.00 (2)
Zinfandel,'87, Santa Cruz Mtns., Vineyard Hill, Estate (S-Orange)

YORK MOUNTAIN WINERY

York Mtn. Road, W. Templeton CA 93465

Cabernet Sauvignon,'86, San Luis Obispo $15.00 (B-San Fran)

Merlot,'87, San Luis Obispo $16.00 (3)
Pinot Noir,'87, Central Coast $12.00 (B-San Fran)
Zinfandel,'87, San Luis Obispo $9.00 (2)

Z

Z. MOORE WINERY
3364 River Road Windsor CA 95492
Gewurztraminer,'89, Carneros, SLH $7.50 (2)
Gewurztraminer,'89, Russian River Vly. $8.50 (3)
Zinfandel,'88, Sonoma Co. $11.00 (B-State Fair)

ZACA MESA WINERY
Foxen Canyon Rd. Los Olivos CA 93441
Cabernet Sauvignon,'87, Central Coast, Reserve $18.00 (3)
Cabernet Sauvignon,'87, Santa Barbara Co. (S-Orange)
Chardonnay,'88, Santa Barbara (B-San Diego)
Chardonnay,'88, Santa Barbara Reserve $16.50 (2)
Chardonnay,'89, Santa Barbara Co. $11.00 (2)
Pinot Noir,'88, Santa Barbara Co. (S-W.Coast)
Pinot Noir,'88, Santa Barbara Co., Reserve (3)
Sauvignon Blanc,'89, Santa Barbara $7.75 (B-San Fran)
White Zinfandel,'89, Santa Barbara Co. (B-Dallas)

ZD WINES
8383 Silverado Trail Napa CA 94558
Cabernet Sauvignon,'86, Napa Vly. $16.00 (3)
Chardonnay,'88, California $20.00 (4)
Pinot Noir,'86, Napa Vly., Carneros (S-San Diego)

STEPHEN ZELLERBACH
4611 Thomas Road Healdsburg CA 95448
Chardonnay,'88, Sonoma $8.00 (3)
Sauvignon Blanc,'89, Sonoma $5.00 (B-San Fran)

Tasting Notes

Tasting Notes

Tasting Notes

Tasting Notes

Tasting Notes

Tasting Notes

Please send me the current *CWW*. I have last year's book and use it <u>all</u> the time. Many thanks for this guide!

Bonita, CA

..I feel that I have saved the purchase price on each bottle of wine I have bought.... I never go wine shopping without it.

Houston

I've been hoping you would publish it again this year, so I was delighted to receive your letter. Thanks!

Tulare, CA

I've thoroughly enjoyed your 1984 edition. It is very helpful in purchasing quality wines. I'm looking forward to receiving the 1985 edition.

Pittsburgh, PA

How could anyone who collects and cellars California wines be without it? Thanks!

Ojai, CA

We are importers of California wines into Europe and have great use for your '83 and '84 *CWW*. ...send us a copy of the '85 and two of the '86 when it is ready...

Floda, Sweden

Please rush a copy of your most recent edition of *CWW*. I'm up against a deadline...

Fullerton, CA

...it was helpful in picking many great wines for our cellar.

Menlo Park, CA